Juvenile Justice

Juvenile Justice

Laura L. Finley

Historical Guides to Controversial Issues in America

GREENWOOD PRESS
Westport, Connecticut • London

Library of Congress Cataloging-in-Publication Data

Finley, Laura L.
    Juvenile justice / Laura L. Finley.
        p. cm. — (Historical guides to controversial issues in America, ISSN 1541–0021)
    Includes bibliographical references and index.
    ISBN-13: 978–0–313–33882–3 (alk. paper)   1. Juvenile justice,
Administration of—United States—History.   I. Title.
    HV9104.F53   2007
    364.360973—dc22   2007018354

British Library Cataloguing in Publication Data is available.

Library of Congress Catalog Card Number: 2007018354
ISBN-13: 978–0–313–33882–3
ISSN: 1541–0021

First published in 2007

Greenwood Press, 88 Post Road West, Westport, CT 06881
An imprint of Greenwood Publishing Group, Inc.
www.greenwood.com

Printed in the United States of America

The paper used in this book complies with the
Permanent Paper Standard issued by the National
Information Standards Organization (Z39.48–1984).

10 9 8 7 6 5 4 3 2 1

Contents

Preface: Conceptual Overview and Organization of the Book

Americans have always held a complex mix of feelings about children and adolescents. There are two primary attitudes about young people: fear *for* them—for their safety, their well being, their opportunities for success, and so on—and fear *of* them. The history of childhood is a "double image," vacillating between "child as devil and as adult."[1] Most people hold both feelings simultaneously, although which one dominates varies with sociocultural changes. One historian explained, "Americans are deeply ambivalent about children. Adults envy young people their youth, vitality, and physical attractiveness. But they also resent children's intrusions on their time and resources and frequently fear their passions and drives."[2] This book is a history of juvenile justice. Yet juvenile justice is a very broad concept, encompassing everything from the making of law at the front end to corrections on the back end. As such, this book is focused on examining a specific conceptual debate that permeates how the juvenile justice system operates. This book explores the competing attitudes about young people held throughout the history of the United States, and how these have influenced juvenile justice.

Early American colonists inherited this ambivalence about youth from their European predecessors. In general, Europeans prior to the Enlightenment felt young people were no different than adults and thus required no different care or treatment after the age of six or seven. The first colonists, according to most histories, felt the same. Yet despite this apparently harsh view, there is evidence of more loving and nurturing attitudes. Most parents loved their children and were devastated when disease or disaster struck their children.[3]

As the fledgling nation grew larger with a more diverse population, and as new technologies were developed to alter daily living, the trend in attitudes toward young people shifted. Although many still saw young people as more burden than blessing, reformers in the 1800s began to advocate a more nurturing approach. Still, even as nurturing came to be the buzzword for treatment of children and adolescents, history tells another story. Rather than being seen as valuable human beings in their own right, adults still often feared youth. This trend continues to this day.

Despite claims to understand them better through the still developing fields of psychology, sociology, and social work, adults did not, and arguably still do not, truly "get" young people. Perhaps this is because young people have not had—still do not have—much voice in the United States. The very youngest cannot explain themselves well, and even when children are able to articulate their feelings, few adults listen. This disparity may also have to do with Americans' general inability to "walk in another person's shoes." Or, perhaps it is as Albert Memmi maintained—the oppressed become the oppressor.[4] This quote sums it up nicely: "It's as if most adults, having endured childhood, want nothing more to do with it until they can enforce its constraints on their own children in their own way. Even though we have all been children, as adults we do not, as a rule, remember clearly the feelings associated with that stage of our lives or empathize with young people currently undergoing that stage."[5]

Regardless of the reasons, what we do not understand, we tend to fear. What we fear are things that must be controlled. Although it is easy to convince everyone that certain populations must be controlled—prisoners, for instance—it is not always so easy to "sell" control of seemingly innocent populations. Thus, oftentimes control of innocent populations is couched in paternalistic logic. Rather than control, it is called "concern" or "help." Populations receiving these "good works" are told to praise the benevolent ones who bestow it upon them, lauding their grace and trusting them to do best. Hence woven throughout the "modern" history of attitudes toward children and adolescents in the United States is a thread of social control efforts designed for "their own good."[6] Although sometimes it might be partially true that most social control mechanisms do *some* good, too often, these efforts are more harmful than helpful. In all cases, they assume an inability of the targeted population to direct and control their own lives. "We persist in the notion that adults, on the whole, have children's best interests at heart, and that they will act on behalf of those interests. We avoid the reality that both parents and the state often put their own interests first and neglect those of children, especially when the two sets of interests conflict."[7]

All types of institutions in which youth are involved have and still do reflect the ambivalence about youth. Policy, too, is "for their own good." Because policymakers say a policy or practice is designed to help young people, we, as a public, typically believe them. Rarely do we question whether young people are truly "helped" or whether there might be other, better, ways to "help." Although we are not overtly "pro-abuse," "our society engages in cultural policies and perpetuates cultural myths that promote the abuses we claim to abhor. Our head says no, but our hands say yes."[8] The situation is far worse when it interacts with a variety of "isms"—racism, sexism, nationalism, and ethnocentrism make it all too easy for middle-class white adults to manage minority young people "for their own good."

Policies and practices that emanate from fear *of* or fear *for* youth have become common sense; they are just the way we do things. Theorists on punishment have called these instituted ways of doing things "regimes of truth."[9] The following quote summarizes how we fail to recognize the harm in our policies and practices.

The forces working against children's interests are subtle and disguised to the point of being practically invisible; they are rooted less in conscious antagonism than in unconscious conceptual frameworks. The disconnect between our apparently child-centered culture and our treatment of individual children stems in part from the fact that we do not see children as a social group with a distinct political status. Our culture categorizes young people into our own children, other people's children, ourselves as children, bad children, etc.[10]

Our ambivalence about children and youth has significant consequences. The ways youth are (mis)treated impacts their attitudes toward authority.[11] Further, policies based in fear, either of or for, prevent us from developing truly effective ways of raising new generations. Another scholar elaborated, "As long as children are viewed as animals that need to be tamed and diseases that need to be quarantined, adult hostility will thrive and adult compassion for children's difficult, adult-orchestrated circumstances will be hard to come by."[12]

Although the ambivalence about youth permeates all social institutions, it is perhaps most clearly demonstrated in the juvenile justice system. Here, we see how adults have crafted policies that at times reflect great love and concern. The reformers who created the juvenile court system, for instance, certainly *felt* they were helping young people. And, in many ways, they were—their fear *for* the health and well-being led them to institute a number of protective measures. At the same time, these policies show a lack of understanding and often tremendous fear of young people. The result is an institution that is a panoply of mixed messages. Indeed, some scholars today say the system is unrecognizable from the system that was intended. These critics contend the system is too broken to be fixed and might as well be discarded. Others maintain it *could* be fixed, but to do so would necessitate a dramatic shift in attitudes about juveniles. This book does not take a position on that particular debate, per se; rather, my intent is to offer a history of juvenile justice in the United States that highlights the opposing attitudes adults hold of youth. It is intended to be a resource for those interested in understanding the pros and cons of taking either a parental or a punitive approach to juvenile justice, in each of their many manifestations.

This controversy is critical for a number of reasons. First, crime is a major social issue, and research has repeatedly documented that juvenile crime specifically troubles the public. In particular, people fear violent crime perpetrated by juveniles. School violence received a great deal of attention in the later 1990s. There is a large and growing body of literature documenting that the American public significantly overestimates the incidence of violent crime perpetrated by juveniles. While schools remain one of the safest places for juveniles, for instance—chances of a teenager being killed in school are one in 2 million—research after the Columbine shooting found 71 percent of Americans believed a similar attack was "likely" or "very likely" in their schools.[13] Because of this fear of juvenile crime, the ways this country should treat juvenile offenders is a matter of great public concern.

Second, treating juvenile offenders costs a great deal of money, so ascertaining the most effective method is a fiscally responsible goal. One report calculated that it costs $43,000 per year to incarcerate a juvenile offender, which averages to $117 per day. Clearly, that figure does not consider the many other costs of juvenile delinquency, in particular the vast amount of indirect costs.

Third, as the world becomes more global, it is imperative that the United States considers how responses to juvenile offenders may be viewed on the international scene. For instance, the United States is the only industrialized country that has yet to sign the United Nations Convention on the Rights of the Child. After examining these attitudes and the ways they have manifested in juvenile justice, perhaps it will be possible to move forward with a more just, humane, and useful method of dealing with delinquent and needy youth.

This book documents two things: Historical attitudes toward young people, and how those attitudes translated into policy and practice with delinquent youth. It is not intended to be a textbook that documents all the practices and procedures in juvenile justice. As the reader will see, the chapters do provide an overview of how the system works, but this overview is not necessarily a detailed procedural model of the courts. Nor is the book meant to be an in-depth examination of any specific issue in juvenile justice, any delinquency theory, any legal concern, or any particular era. Readers will find pieces about theories that were influential in the decade(s) discussed in every chapter, but these are included to frame the presentation of that era's fear *of* versus fear *for* manifestation. As such, it is not meant to be a reader on theory. Likewise, some significant court cases and legal changes are addressed, but these are not covered exhaustively. In sum, this book is meant to be a summation of how beliefs over time have contributed to a system of mixed messages and procedures.

Although this book is focused on the United States, it is useful to briefly examine how the original colonists derived their understanding of childhood and adolescence and the ways they dealt with delinquent juveniles. The Introduction begins with a brief overview of "juvenile justice" in Europe. Juvenile justice is in quotations because it will soon become clear that no real system existed. However, the chapter includes several signs indicating that many did indeed understand juveniles to be different from adults. Europeans' attitudes passed on to those in the colonies, and institutions from Europe were re-created and revamped in the new territory. Further, while treatment of delinquents and wayward youth was notoriously harsh, the chapter makes clear that ripples of softer attitudes can be identified. The Introduction is organized with the material demonstrating harsh attitudes first, followed by the evidence of more temperate views.

Chapter 1 explores the shifts in attitudes and policies that accompanied the dramatic expansion and development of the United States. It highlights how reformers in the eighteenth and nineteenth centuries studied, understood, and responded to juvenile delinquency. This time is called the early Progressive era. These progressive so-called child savers are both commended and deplored for the juvenile justice system they created. Chapter 1 also explores early theories regarding adolescent crime and adolescent development that were integral in the creation of the juvenile system. In addition, the chapter describes the opposition to the creation of a separate system for juveniles.

Chapter 2 covers the latter part of the Progressive era, examining in more detail the court system that was created at the turn of the twentieth century. The chapter presents both the innovations included in the earliest juvenile courts as well as the earliest problems identified. The chapter covers trends in juvenile justice until the start of the 1920s. As such, it briefly addresses the impact of World War I. Additionally, it presents information about important social trends, including anti-immigrant sentiment and the growth of the eugenics movement.

Chapter 3 follows the development of the juvenile justice system, examining how competing attitudes about youth shaped the system from the 1920s through the 1950s. It stresses the important cases, events, and legislation that shaped the developing juvenile system, as well as the competing views on how to treat juveniles. Special attention will be given to developing theories in child and adolescent development as well as in criminology that contributed to the growth of juvenile courts modeled on *parens patriae.*

Chapter 4 looks at the dramatic changes occurring in juvenile justice between the 1960s and 1980s, and how these can be viewed as both helpful and harmful to young people. The liberal era of the 1960s emphasized social conditions as the roots of crime and deviance and supported use of rehabilitation with both juvenile and adult offenders. It was at this time that many people began to question the ethics and utility of incarceration, as well as the impact it might have on youth who were labeled delinquent. The chapter describes important developments in adolescent psychology and in criminology that impacted views and treatment of juvenile offenders. Also addressed is an examination of important political trends of the era that contributed to the implementation of a number of social programs, as well as the support for and opposition to these initiatives.

As crime began to be a focus of presidential campaigning, the end of the era signaled a shift toward a "get tough" approach that moved juvenile justice closer to adult justice. In the mid-1970s and the 1980s, challenges to the ideals of juvenile justice began to dismantle the system. Important developments, such as increased use of crime as a political tool, economic depression, the war on drugs, rising gang membership, and the explosion of the "crack epidemic," are briefly discussed to highlight the beginning of a more punitive trend in juvenile justice.

Chapter 5 examines the punitive era of the late 1980s through the present. In doing so, it evaluates the pros and cons of many of the most current developments in juvenile justice, including the increased use of incarceration and detention (both pre-adjudication and in sentencing), use of waivers to adult court, zero tolerance laws, curfews for juveniles, the juvenile death penalty, and many more. Further, the chapter pays special attention to the public perception of juvenile crime, stressing how misperceptions were often used to justify more severe punishments. In addition, this chapter includes information about school violence and responses to it, as the 1990s saw tremendous public concern about the safety of schools. The chapter highlights the introduction of a number of developmental theories of delinquency at the time the punitive trend was occurring that are less about blaming and more about understanding. While a punitive trend was continuing, some states were dramatically overhauling their entire juvenile justice system to represent new, more therapeutic thinking. Community-based programs, like Boston's Operation Ceasefire, represented almost a return to earlier decades of community building.

Building on the previous chapter, Chapter 6 examines evidence of a continuation of the punitive trend, such as the increased access to juvenile files, as well as evidence of a more therapeutic approach, such as the incorporation of a restorative justice model and the development of youth courts. In particular, laws dealing with juvenile sex offenders and use of boot camps are highlighted. The chapter also discusses some of the most salient concerns with juvenile justice, including abuse in detention, how to work with juvenile suffering from mental illness, and the mental capacity of juveniles to understand their rights.

NOTES

1. deMause, L. (1988). The evolution of childhood. In L. deMause (Ed.). *The history of childhood: the untold story of child abuse* (pp. 1–73). New York: Peter Bedrick Books, p. 21.

2. Mintz, S. (2004). *Huck's raft: A history of American childhood.* Cambridge, MA: The Belknap Press of Harvard University Press, p.2.

3. Slater, P. (1985). "From the *cradle* to the *coffin*": Parental bereavement and the shadow of infant damnation in Puritan society. In N. Hiner & J. Hawes (Eds.). *Growing up in America: Children in historical perspective* (pp. 27–45). Urbana, IL: University of Chicago Press.

4. Memmi, A. (1965). *The colonizer and the colonized.* Boston, MA: Beacon.

5. Hodgson, L. (1997). *Raised in captivity: Why does America fail its children?* Saint Paul, MN: Graywolf Press, p. 5.

6. Miller, A. (1983). For your own good: Hidden cruelty in childrearing and the roots of Violence (3rd ed.). New York: Farrar, Straus and Giroux.

7. Hodgson (1997), p. 11.

8. Ibid., p. 63.

9. Garland, D. (1990). *Punishment and modern society.* Chicago, IL: University of Chicago Press.

10. Hodgson (1997), p. 94.

11. Greven, P. (1990). *Spare the child.* New York: Vintage.

12. Hodgson (1997), p. 197.

13. Newman, K. (2004). *Rampage.* New York: Basic.

Acknowledgments

Any work of this length and depth involves many people, either directly or indirectly. Directly, thanks to all those who provided research assistance in identifying books and articles cited within. This includes my students at Florida Atlantic University as well as my loving husband, Peter.

Indirectly, many others supported me in writing this book. First and foremost, my immediate family—Peter and Anya. Mom's late hours were sometimes a burden, but hopefully the result is a book people will find useful and interesting. Anya (age 3 1/2 at completion) will likely have a perpetual fear of computers, since she heard "do NOT push any buttons!" on a daily basis. Peter has, as always, been a supportive and helpful ally. My love to you both, and to moronic but lovely dogs Sissy and Cliff.

I also wish to acknowledge my employers. While writing this book, I engaged in an experiment of balancing two full-time jobs. I taught sociology courses full-time at Florida Atlantic University at the same time I was Training Manager and later Director of Social Change at Women In Distress of Broward County, Inc. Although no one at either place overtly knew of the hours I put in at home writing, the support I felt when I was at work helped get me through some very long days.

As readers will learn, this book not only discusses juveniles as offenders, but it touches on the importance of recognizing victimization of juveniles. I have had the great pleasure of working at a domestic violence agency in which we help victims of abuse, including young people. Additionally, my role is in community awareness and prevention. To that end, I wish to devote half of all proceeds made from the sale of this book to Women In Distress of Broward County, Inc. I want to close with my favorite quote from Mahatma Gandhi: "We may never know the results of our actions. But if we take no action, there will be no results." I hope readers of this book will be moved to action of some sort.

1

Introduction: Pre-1800s to Early Nineteenth Century

This chapter offers a brief look at attitudes about young people prior to the 1800s and into the early nineteenth century, both in Europe and the American colonies. It also summarizes how wayward and delinquent juveniles were managed in that time period. As described in the Preface, the book is organized in two halves: First is evidence of harsh attitudes and treatments, followed by evidence of more nurturing attitudes and benevolent treatment. This brief overview is intended to document the competition between fear *of* and fear *for* young people that permeated both the attitudes and beliefs of the public, as well as the policies and institutions they created.

THE HARSH REALITY

In the Middle Ages, those who committed a crime not only defied the law, they were said to defy God as well. Punishment for crime was swift and harsh. As such, they were required to atone for their sins, a process called expiation. This often occurred through an ordeal in which the Church subjected the offender to some type of painful, even fatal, test. Some had their arms and legs bound and were thrown into a lake. If they floated to the surface, they were considered innocent. If they remained submerged, they were considered guilty. Mere suspicion of wrongdoing, in particular if the accusation involved sexual activity or witchcraft, was often enough to warrant severe punishment.[1]

This harshness was not reserved for adults. One historian explained, "The history of childhood is a nightmare from which we have only recently begun to awaken. The further back in history one goes, the lower the level of child care, and the more likely children are to be killed, abandoned, beaten, terrorized, and sexually abused."[2] Prior to the Renaissance, experiences were generally not classified by age distinctions. For the most part, children were considered miniature adults who did not require special status in any institution.[3] In regard to crime, if malice could be discerned, subadolescent-aged children could be subject to trial and possibly sentenced to death.[4] For example, a child murderer was hung in 1338 and a 1488 account describes the execution of a nine-year-old for committing murder.[5] In England, children were tried in the central court of London, often called Old Bailey, the same as adults. Records show, however, that few children were actually tried there. Rather, children were typically placed in stocks and whipped for misbehavior.[6]

Like their European predecessors, the colonists authorized many harsh punishments for juvenile offenders. A 1660 Massachusetts Bay Colony law authorized magistrates to invoke sentences of capital punishment for young people. Judges were also encouraged to use their judgment to apply other severe sentences, such as whipping. Lying and failure to observe the Sabbath were also punishable offenses. In 1671, the New Plymouth Colony authorized the death penalty for children above age 16 who cursed or "smited" their natural mother or father.[7] One researcher calculated a total of 114 children under age 16 were put to death in the United States in the nineteenth century, 108 males and 6 females. The most common death-eligible offenses were murder and robbery-murder.[8]

Outside of any formal justice system, families have historically been the primary means of controlling delinquent and wayward youth. In Medieval Europe, the father had ultimate authority, with his wife and children considered no more than property. The earliest colonists spread this patriarchal model to the west. Young people were to be controlled, as they were viewed as a challenge to patriarchal authority. "The patriarchal family was the building block of Puritan society" and received much support from the church.[9] Patriarchal authority can quite easily shift to outright abuse. Many children born before the eighteenth century would today be considered battered.[10] Documents show young people being beaten in Europe and the colonies with various instruments, including whips, shovels, cans, rods, sticks, and specially made instruments. No real organized attempts to limit the beating of children occurred prior to the eighteenth century. As beating became less popular, however, parents found other means of punishment, including shutting children in dark places.[11]

Like today, parents who disciplined their children with cruelty often offered religious justifications, and claimed to be doing so to "help" their children. The most commonly invoked phrase is the well-known biblical aphorism, "He that spareth his rod hateth his son: but he that loveth him chasteneth him betimes."[12] Puritans viewed infants as sinners, thus those who were disciplining them were really assisting the children in achieving redemption. Reverend Benjamin Wadsworth referred to babies as, "filthy, guilty, odious, abominable ... both by nature and practice."[13] Puritan Preacher Cotton Mather argued that children were, "Better whipt, than damned."[14] Mather described children as sinners, saying, "Are they *Young?* Yet the *Devil* has been with them already ... They go astray as soon as they are born."[15] Childhood was not a time for frivolity and indulgence; rather, it was viewed as a critical period in formulating adults who would maintain an orderly society.[16]

Treatment of the "other"—Native Americans, African slaves, and poor children—was even harsher. Massachusetts and other colonies had laws regarding indentured servants and apprentices that allowed masters to use the courts to punish youth who fornicated, attempted to marry, or gambled.[17] Poor children fared worse than their more affluent peers, and those without parents suffered the most. For those who had no family, a system of "binding out" was implemented, whereby poor children would be apprenticed for specified periods to farmers or into domestic service.[18] Between 1500 and 1620, a 50 percent decline in real wages prompted many others to seek apprenticeships as well. Binding out was also used with those perceived to be out of their family's control. Additionally, children determined to be abused or neglected were often apprenticed.

Apprenticed children were often subject to great cruelty and abuse, although excessive abuse could be brought before the courts. One historian documented a 1660 case in which a young orphan apprentice in Maryland had a "rotten filthy, stinking, ulcerated leg" from abuse.[19] As more youth left the home, youthful vagrancy and delinquency increased.[20] The response was to exercise greater control. In 1672, Massachusetts passed a statute forbidding young people from walking in streets and fields on weekends, a precursor to the curfew laws in later times. The increased anxiety that children would abandon their morality also led to the institution of tithing men, who were charged with regulating youth behavior.[21]

Many slave masters invoked rules authorizing the punishment of slaves. Whipping was common, and mutilation was not unheard of. As historian L. Fishman explained, "Punishment was meted to female slaves regardless of motherhood, pregnancy, or physical injury."[22] Female slaves also suffered from sexual oppression because they were seen as "breeders." Masters raped female slaves young and old, as well as rented or borrowed men for "stud services" and sold young slaves as prostitutes.[23] Some responded to this treatment by committing a number of criminal acts, including anything from the relatively mundane stealing from their masters to the far more serious assault, murder, and infanticide.[24]

Women and girls were, according to the Puritans, naturally more evil than men and thus were in need of taming. Laws authorized men to beat their spouses and their daughters as long as the curtains were drawn and with rods and switches no bigger than the circumference of their thumb—the Rule of the Curtains and the Rule of Thumb. The Puritans believed young women to be especially susceptible to the evil of witchcraft. All kinds of crimes were blamed on female witches, exemplified most notably by the Salem Witch Trials of 1692.[25] Ultimately, most scholars assert the witch trials were about a desire to control women.[26] In opposition to these punitive trends, however, history documents a more nurturing approach with young people.

PATERNALISTIC VIEWS AND POLICIES

As early as the mid-eighteenth century, French philosopher Jean-Jacques Rousseau recognized children to be creative creatures with wisdom to share with their elders.[27] Rousseau's *Emile,* as well as widely read fiction by Daniel Defoe and others, questioned the patriarchal family as repressive and offered the idea that parents could rear children through love, rather than coercion.[28] John Locke also recommended that, because children were a blank slate, their nurture was critical. Scottish philosopher Francis Hutcheson offered the idea that children have rights and should be considered more than simply the property of their parents.[29]

Although it is true that adolescents were seen as generally the same as adults, there were early signs of understanding that perhaps different treatment was required with youth. In particular, this was true of criminal justice. The London Bridewell of 1555 is considered the first institution designed to control young beggars and vagrants. In 1576, Parliament enacted legislation to create a Bridewell in every county. Certainly these institutions were not about fun and games, but set an important precedent that young delinquents should and could be dealt with separate from adult offenders. Young inmates in Bridewells were made to work, which was said to foster industriousness that they were to use in the labor force upon release. Sometimes parents placed their own children in Bridewells, believing the work regimen would help their child.[30] One of the first prisons in the world was designed specifically for juveniles. In 1704, Pope Clement XI built the Hospice at San

Michele in Rome. The facility housed both those sentenced for actual crimes and "incorrigible" youth.[31]

The earliest court precedent that juveniles should be treated different from adults in court came from the 1721 English case of *Duke of Beaufort v. Berty.* Not long after, an English court precedent, *Rex v. Deleval* in 1763, established the notion of individualized justice for youth.[32] The principle legal justification for most of the early efforts to separate juveniles from adults was the doctrine of *parens patriae.* Originating in medieval England, *parens patriae* authorized the Crown to intervene in a family's affairs when a child's welfare was threatened.[33] Initially applied only in cases involving affluent families, the doctrine soon spread across England and was affirmed in the 1827 *Wellesley* decision.[34] Interestingly, some believe *parens patriae* originated from an error in English Chancery courts, in which a printer accidentally substituted the word *enfant* for *ideot.*[35]

The philosophy of *parens patriae* exemplifies the "for your own good" approach. While they held the negative views of young people, Puritans, by and large, cared deeply about their children. In fact, many made the perilous trip across the Atlantic solely because they felt America would be a good place to raise their children.[36] According to one historian, "Most parents in eighteenth-century Virginia and Maryland were deeply attached to their children and they structured family life around them."[37]

In addition, Puritan authors published numerous volumes on childrearing and were the first group to maintain that entire communities, not just families, were responsible for children's upbringing.[38] Because males were the heads of families, childrearing manuals were directed to fathers, not mothers.[39] Fathers, according to some scholars, were more emotionally involved with their children at an early age than many are today.[40]

Many Puritans were also highly critical of excessive punishment, arguing that parents should always explain the reasons for punishment and never use it arbitrarily, capriciously, or with anger.[41] Not all colonial families believed in the "spare the rod" approach. Most notably, Native families rejected the use of harsh physical punishments. They also rejected the use of threats and coercion, preferring gentle words to guide problem youth.[42]

The laws of Massachusetts did recognize age differences among offenders, just not to the degree we do today. For many crimes, 14 was the age at which a child could be executed, rather than "punished severely."[43] Even the Massachusetts Bay "stubborn child law," widely cited for authorizing the death penalty in cases when children disobey parents, was innovative because it recognized children as distinct from adults and it recognized parental authority, but at the same time, it recognized when the state could intervene with the family.[44] The stubborn child law foreshadowed the 1838 case of *ex Parte Crouse,* which affirmed use of *parens patriae* with troublesome children.

As the United States shifted from being largely agricultural to urban and industrial, young people took on different economic roles and a different social and legal status. The period of childhood was extended, and children were economically dependent upon parents for far longer time periods.[45] Parents were assigned greater responsibility for rearing their children "appropriately."[46] Appropriate childrearing was shifting from fear *of* to fear *for.*

Parents supervised their children closely to inculcate moral character, economic diligence, appropriate manners, sexual modesty, obedience and respect for adult authority and self control. By the turn of the century, the idealized conception of childhood provided a benchmark by which to measure parental success and a standard against which to evaluate children's deviance.[47]

Because middle- and upper-class women tended to have greater education, and their economic status allowed them greater opportunities to stay home with children, they were perceived as being better parents.[48] Other social classes and ethnic groups did not, or in some cases could not, prescribe to the same philosophy of childrearing.[49]

The Revolutionary War also prompted new attitudes about young people. Children were seen as essential in establishing and preserving the new republic. Dr. Benjamin Rush, a signatory to the Declaration of Independence, expressed the need for parenting and schooling to maintain social stability. Rush declared, "Mothers and school-masters plant the seeds of nearly all the good and evil which exist in our world."[50] The emphasis on the role of the mother was novel; although women had long been responsible for the daily care of children, males were the head of the family, and thus childrearing was seen as their domain. The new ideal of childhood drew on the earlier writings of Romantics, such as Rousseau and Locke, who stressed that children were distinct from adults. To protect their innocence, children were to be separated from adult problems. This attitude prompted the construction of a number of institutions for children, including public schools, Sunday schools, orphanages, and hospitals.[51]

In sum, the brief history presented in this chapter shows two competing views of young people. Although young people were viewed with condescension and disbelief,[52] they were also viewed with love and awe.[53] Puritans tended to see deviance as an individual defect.[54] At the same time, the Puritans universalized deviance.[55] In doing so, they rarely authorized the most serious sanctions allowable by their own laws and mentioned in the Bible. Puritans saw deviance and misbehavior everywhere, and their first attempt to deal with delinquency was to control it systematically, as with the stubborn child laws. In the event this did not work, they responded with "hysterical abandon, as in the witch trials."[56] The goal was not simply repression, but rather "internalized repression."[57]

Toward the end of the eighteenth century, explanations for crime began to change. One of the most important influences on criminal justice and juvenile justice in the United States emerged in Europe. Known as the Classical School of Criminology, the theory suggested people freely choose to commit crime. The person most commonly associated with the classical school is French author and scholar Cesare Beccaria. Beccaria first outlined his ideas on crime in 1764 in his book, *On Crimes and Punishment*. Beccaria maintained that people have free will and they choose their behaviors based on an evaluation of the pleasures they might derive and the pain they might incur. Initially, Beccaria's work was interpreted to mean all humans, regardless of their age, mental capacity, or intellect, are able to reason and act on their own free will. In 1791, France enacted a Penal Code based on this notion. It quickly became clear to policymakers, however, that this assumption was not entirely true. Perhaps some people simply do not weigh things the same way, or perhaps legitimate opportunities are limited for certain demographic groups. Beccaria also did not specify precisely how much and what kinds of pleasures or pains were required to influence an individual to offend. Revisions were made to the Penal Code to account for some of these issues, including the recognition of mitigating factors that might influence someone's ability to reason.[58]

A proponent of Beccaria's ideas was Jeremy Bentham, who in 1789 authored *An Introduction to the Principles of Morals and Legislation*. Bentham generally agreed that offenders operate on the pleasure principle, but furthered the notion that a community or society must consider mitigating factors in order to achieve the greatest happiness and safety for the largest number of people.[59] Because he recognized the role of mitigating and extenuating circumstances, Bentham is often called a neoclassical theorist. The development of unique services for juveniles, especially a court designed only to hear cases involving youth, is a result of Bentham's views. Age is one of the most significant mitigating factors in determining both guilt as well as sentencing.[60]

As this chapter made clear, most of the institutions created to deal with delinquent youth in these eras operated from the harsher view, yet there were always glimpses of more gentle approaches. Both approaches have a legacy today. Likewise, the attitude that juveniles choose to commit crime remains, and the debate over whether they can developmentally understand the consequences of their actions continues as well. The stubborn child law remained in force, albeit in amended form, until 1973. Further, "the

Puritan notion of legal child regulation was never entirely extinguished."[61] As the nineteenth century approached, new ideas about parenting spawned new institutions as well. These new attitudes and institutions may have been slightly less harsh, at least physically, but they did not offer juveniles a voice of their own, nor did they care for all young people the same. Women, poor children, and racial minorities were subject to far greater controls and crueler treatment. *Parens patriae* ushered in a new form of "for their own good" approaches that set the stage for later juvenile justice initiatives, including the juvenile courts.

NOTES

1. Vito, G., & Simonson, C. (2004). *Juvenile justice today* (4th ed.). Upper Saddle River, NJ: Prentice Hall.

2. deMause, L. (1988). The evolution of childhood. In L. deMause (Ed.). *The history of childhood: The untold story of child abuse* (pp. 1–73). New York: Peter Bedrick Books, p. 1.

3. Feld, B. (1999). *Bad kids: Race and the transformation of the juvenile court.* New York: Oxford University Press.

4. Watkins, J. (1998). *The juvenile justice century.* Durham, NC: Carolina Academic Press.

5. Ibid.

6. Vito & Simonson (2004).

7. Watkins (1998).

8. Ibid.

9. Mintz, S. (2004). *Huck's raft: A history of American childhood.* Cambridge, MA: The Belknap Press of Harvard University Press, p. 13.

10. deMause, (1988).

11. Ibid.

12. Cited in Greven, P. (1990). *Spare the child.* New York: Vintage, p. 48.

13. Mintz (2004), p. 11.

14. Youcha, G. (1995). *Minding the children: Child care in America from colonial times to the present.* New York: Scribner, p. 35.

15. Mintz (2004), p. 11.

16. Ibid.

17. Lerman, P. (1991). Delinquency and social policy: A historical perspective. In E. Monkkonen (Ed.), *Crime & justice in American history: Delinquency and disorderly behavior* (pp. 23–33). Westport, CT: Meckler Publishing.

18. Krisberg, B., & Austin, J. (1993). *Reinventing juvenile justice.* Newbury Park, CA: Sage.

19. Youcha (1995), p. 36.

20. Mintz (2004).

21. Ibid.

22. Fishman, L. (2003). "Mule-headed slave woman refusing to take foolishness from anybody": A prelude to future accommodation, resistance, and criminality. In R. Muraskin (Ed.), *It's a crime* (3rd ed, pp. 30–49). Upper Saddle River, NJ: Prentice Hall, p. 33.

23. Ibid.

24. Ibid.

25. Wilson, N. (2003). Taming women and nature: The criminal justice system and the creation of crime in Salem Village. In R. Muraskin (Ed.), *It's a crime* (3rd ed., pp. 3–11). Upper Saddle River, NJ: Prentice Hall.

26. Erikson, K. (1966). *Wayward Puritans.* New York: Wiley.

27. Sealander, J. (2003). *The failed century of the child.* Cambridge: Cambridge University Press.

28. Mintz (2004).

29. Ibid.

30. Krisberg & Austin (1993).

31. Vito & Simonson (2004).

32. Ibid.

33. Schlossman, S. (1977). *Love and the American delinquent.* Chicago: University of Chicago Press.

34. Ibid.

35. Rendleman, D. (1991). Parens patriae: From chancery to the juvenile court. In E. Monkkonen (Ed.), *Crime & justice in American history: Delinquency and disorderly behavior* (pp. 119–173). Westport, CT: Meckler Publishing, p. 121.

36. Mintz (2004).

37. Smith, D. (1985). Autonomy and affection: Parents and children in eighteenth-century Chesapeake families. In N. Hiner & J. Hawes (Eds.), *Growing up in America: Children in historical perspective* (pp. 45–60). Urbana, IL: University of Chicago Press, p. 45.

38. Mintz (2004).

39. Ibid.

40. Smith (1985).

41. Mintz (2004).

42. Ibid.

43. Beales, R. (1985). In search of the historical child: Miniature adulthood and youth in colonial New England. In N. Hiner & J. Hawes (Eds.), *Growing up in America: Children in historical perspective* (pp. 7–26). Urbana, IL: University of Chicago Press, p. 12.

44. Sutton, J. (1988). *Stubborn children.* Berkeley, CA: University of California Press.

45. Feld (1999).

46. Ibid.

47. Ibid, p. 30.

48. Ibid.

49. Ibid.

50. Mintz (2004), p. 71.

51. Ibid.

52. Beales (1985).

53. Slater, P. (1985). "From the *cradle* to the *coffin*": Parental bereavement and the shadow of infant damnation in Puritan society. In N. Hiner & J. Hawes (Eds.), *Growing up in America: Children in historical perspective* (pp. 27–45). Urbana, IL: University of Chicago Press.

54. Erikson (1966).

55. Sutton (1988).

56. Ibid., p. 39.

57. Ibid., p. 41.

58. Shoemaker, D. (1996). *Theories of delinquency* (3rd ed.). New York: Oxford University Press.

59. Ibid.

60. Ibid.

61. Sutton (1988), p. 42.

2

Early Progressive Era

In the mid-1800s, obvious examples of progressive attitudes and disciplinary approaches toward youth emerged. These approaches emphasized the distinctions between children and adults and the need for care and nurture of young people. The nineteenth century is considered the "century of childhood."[1] Children were perceived as being different from and more innocent than adults. The second half of the nineteenth century, from about 1850 until 1890, has been called the era of the child savers. Although similar in most respects to early reformers, child savers generally had more confidence in their ability to reform wayward juveniles.[2] According to historian Anthony Platt, what differentiated the child saver movement from earlier efforts was the widespread recognition that significant social, political, and economic reforms were needed.[3] Child savers created many organizations and policies that, at least in theory, addressed the needs of young people. For instance, a key organization involved in the awareness of youth delinquency as a social problem was the Society for the Prevention of Pauperism (SPPP), formed in New York City in 1817. In 1822, the SPPP issued a report calling for the creation of special prisons for youth offenders.[4]

The 40-year period between 1880 and 1920 is widely known as the Progressive Era (Watkins, 1998). Although innovative in many ways, this "progress" was not always good. On the positive side, progressives addressed a variety of social issues, including social welfare and political and economic reform.[5]

Still, more negative attitudes and punitive approaches remained, even among those dedicated to "helping" juvenile delinquents. Out of this era, innovations such as indeterminate sentencing, public defenders, professional police, extensive use of parole, mental and IQ testing, and the scientific study of crime emerged.[6] Rather than alter social structures, Progressives sought to "minister" to offenders.[7] In particular, attitudes about and treatment of poor young people, racial minorities, and females demonstrated that little had changed but the packaging. "Law and practice enforced the 'work ethic' harshly on poor children in early America ... Being 'tightfisted' toward the children of the poor was long regarded as a virtue, and reforms for poor children were couched in moralistic terms. Saving children through charity, protecting morality through discipline, and providing safeguards for property provided the yeast for the recipe."[8]

While Progressives tried to "help" young people and their families, they also sought to preserve the existing class system and distribution of wealth that in general favored them. During this era, those in positions of power feared the urban masses would destroy the wealth they had built. Platt argued, "The child-saving movement was not simply a humanistic enterprise on behalf of the lower classes against the established order. On the contrary, its impetus came primarily from the middle and upper classes, who were instrumental in developing new forms of social control to protect their privileged positions in American society."[9] Historian S. Mintz explained,

An underlying ambiguity marked these child-saving efforts. They attempted both to protect children from the dangers of urban society and to protect society from dangerous children. Many child-savers were guilty of paternalism, class and racial bias, xenophobia, and double standards regarding gender. They often confused delinquency and neglect with the realities of life under poverty.[10]

BASIC BELIEFS OF REFORMERS

Reformers claimed that government would be more moral if it was more rational, rather than more Christian, as earlier reformers had advocated.[11] Barry Feld maintains that Progressives were committed to rationality, or the belief that experts and professionals, utilizing "objective" scientific methods, could alleviate social ills.[12] Progressives felt that the scientific method could solve all social problems, which required careful observation and clarification of facts, and the reliance on experts to do so as well. "Investigation was not enough. Experts, reformers felt, should control the public welfare."[13] The child savers were far more inclined to believe experts and to advocate for greater state intervention than earlier reformers.[14] Many of the Progressives were graduates of new universities who had been taught that scientific methods could help understand and ameliorate problematic social conditions.[15]

This belief in the role of experts and professionals resulted in a gradual shift of the locus of control for delinquency, from parenting to greater state intervention.[16] Both the charity movements and the courts movements were guided by this alleged scientific and moral ideology. Yet, "the 'scientific' criteria by which aid was offered consistently revealed implicit moral judgments: the home is superior to the institution; sobriety is better than drunkenness; and a job is more helpful than the dole. The Progressive charity worker, like the Progressive political reformer, could not quite believe that the poor were capable of making decisions regarding their own welfare."[17]

Another effect of the so-called "help" provided by child savers was to widen the net of involvement by and with the state, often in ways that were less than helpful to the youth. Progressive child savers based their strategies on two contradictory notions—while assigning families the primary role for socializing children, Progressives also advocated greater state involvement to oversee this socialization.[18] The Chicago Progressives had a profound faith in government. Government, they agreed, should respond to social problems, and reformers were eager to provide wide discretionary powers to do so.[19] "Reformers regarded minor offenders, un-supervised children, and children of immigrant parents as social victims and appropriate objects of benevolence."[20] Progressives saw the government as a way to spread their values. "The most distinguishing characteristic of the state was to do good. The state was not the enemy of liberty, but the friend of equality—and to expand its domain an increase its power was to be in harmony with the spirit of the age ... the state was not a behemoth to be chained and fettered, but an agent capable of fulfilling an ambitious program."[21]

VIEWS OF DELINQUENTS

Historian J. Sutton (1988) summed up the views of human nature that drove social change in the early nineteenth century.

The first, Calvinism, formed the root stock of American culture, not only in New England, but in areas of Presbyterian influence in the South as well. Enlightenment thought provided the diffuse and plastic vocabulary of American liberalism, a rational framework within which a variety of disparate groups could negotiate their vision of the good life. Romanticism, still nascent in the 1820s and 1830s, was a revolt of the spirit carried out by disaffected intellectuals against the rationalistic scriptures of urban, commercial society.[22]

Child savers viewed delinquents both with contempt and with benevolence. Delinquents were considered less than human, an idea derived from nativist and racist ideologies of the time, including the criminological theory of Cesare Lombroso and the Social Darwinism of Herbert Spencer.[23] One of the most influential theories of the later 1800s was the constitutional criminology of Italian physician Cesare Lombroso. Lombroso posited that offenders were evolutionary throwbacks, or atavists, who were simply less developed than other men. They could be identified by their unique physical characteristics, including their large appendages and asymmetrical heads.[24] The atavists possessed less-developed brains, which made them incapable of conforming to societal norms. Lombroso concluded that female offenders were also atavists and were more masculine than other women. Although Lombroso's work was rife with methodological problems (he primarily studied deceased and executed offenders), it was highly influential at the time.[25] In later decades, Charles Goring and Ernest Hooton both tested Lombroso's theory and claimed to find support for it.[26]

Consistent with these theories, criminals were described as "creatures" who lived in "burrows," and as "little Arabs" who were "shiftless," "ignorant," and "indolent."[27] An early criminological anthropologist, Franz Gall, developed a theory he called phrenology. Gall posited that the shape of the human skull determined a person's personality, and thus their criminality. The concept was that the brain is an organ of the mind and that specific personality characteristics are located at specific parts of the brain. A student of Gall's, Johann Gaspar Spurzheim, brought the idea to America. The notion that crime is rooted in the brain spread through lectures and publications and influenced the early classification systems for prisoners.[28]

Yet, only years later, Progressive court reformers tended to picture juvenile delinquents as innocent and vulnerable children.[29] Later Progressives generally utilized environmental explanations, maintaining crime and deviance were responses to rapid and dramatic social change.[30] Reformers followed the Enlightenment era notion that children were born innocent, as blank slates or *tabula rasa,* and thus their environment was the dominant feature in their delinquency.[31]

In particular, the family was said to be the root cause of criminality. Removing delinquents from these noxious environments and replacing them with strictly disciplined ones was perceived as the best route for reform.[32] In 1877, Richard Dugdale published his study of the Jukes family. He traced the Jukes back to the early 1700s, arguing that, because so many in the family had been involved in crime, it must be genetically linked.[33]

Charles Darwin inaugurated the scientific study of child development in 1877, when he published *A Biographical Sketch of an Infant,* based upon his observations of his son, Doddy, 37 years earlier. Darwin's work inspired a number of systemic studies of mental and emotional development among children.

Other Progressives rejected the idea of social Darwinism. Some focused on the family as the source of degeneracy and poverty, while others stressed broader environmental factors. For instance, Richard Tuthill, a juvenile court judge, said, "a bad home, a bad father, and more surely a bad mother, and want of proper parental care would make delinquents of the children of any one of us."[34] Jane Addams, as well as many others, stressed that the city was the source of physical and moral dangers. Urban delinquency was viewed as the result of teens' search for adventure, and that the temptations of dance halls and saloons were simply too much for some.[35]

Many of the earliest child savers were influenced by the genetic theories promoted by Darwin and Richard Dugdale, although by the late 1890s most tended toward more sociological explanations of delinquency. One of the earliest to recognize the interaction between heredity and environment was Charles Cooley. He observed, "The criminal class is largely the result of society's bad workmanship upon fairly good material," noting there was "a large and trustworthy body of evidence" indicating "degenerates" could be made into "useful citizens."[36]

In 1880, psychologist G. Stanley Hall directed four experienced kindergarten teachers to interview and observe more than 400 Boston area schoolchildren. This study sought to ascertain the level of knowledge students bring with them upon entering school, but the interview and observation model set the stage for future studies of children's development. Throughout the 1880s and 1890s, Hall also enlisted other teachers and mothers to observe their own children and to keep detailed records in hopes of understanding children's development and needs. By the 1910s and 1920s, Hall's work was being criticized for over-reliance on untrained mothers and teachers for the collection of data. Despite these criticisms, the movement was important as a first attempt to study children. Several of these types of studies addressed youth formation of cliques and gangs as well.[37]

The most extreme advocate of scientific childrearing was behavioral psychologist John B. Watson, who believed positive and negative reinforcement modified behavior. Watson argued that, by simply following behaviorist principles, mothers could create any type of child, "A doctor, lawyer, artist, merchant-chief, and yes, even a beggar-man and thief."[38] The scientific form of childrearing came under attack by the later 1920s, most notably by Freudian ideas about the importance of emotions.[39]

Major political, social, and economic events also have a tremendous impact on opinions and policies regarding young people. The next section addresses the impact of the Civil War.

EIGHTEENTH-CENTURY DELINQUENCY AND RESPONSES

The Civil War brought about a change in attitudes regarding children. Mintz explained, "Parents grew more protective of their children, and 'child protection' became a watchword for reform societies seeking to address such social problems as child abuse and neglect."[40] At the same time, capitalist expansion made young people's labor even more valuable. Children of working-class families were especially prone to exploitation, as their families depended on them for economic contributions.[41] Even very young children cut and glued boxes, sewed, and carried goods for businesses. Child laborers faced harsh discipline in the workplace. Most were not hired by the specific mill or factory owner; rather, they were employed by a skilled adult worker. These adult workers ridiculed, taunted, slapped, whipped, and boxed the ears of young workers.[42]

Children of the poorest families often turned to scavenging, which was regarded as petty theft by most of the public. Most children caught by police for scavenging belonged to single-parent homes. Sometimes, if children in these families refused to or were unable to contribute economically, their parent(s) remanded them to authorities or even to state asylums.[43] Certainly, the visual image of poor, scavenging families was unappealing to authorities. "As early as the 1790s, philanthropists and reformers were shocked by the sight of a, 'multitude of half-naked, dirty and leering children' roaming city streets, sleeping in alleyways, picking pockets, and robbing shops. Young girls stood barefoot on street corners, begging for pennies, while small boys picked through garbage scattered in the streets. 'Cunning and adroit,' they bore no resemblance to the middle-class ideal of children as icons of innocence."[44]

It is difficult to find reliable figures on the rates of juvenile violence before, during, and after the Civil War years (1860–1890). There was no uniformly collected criminal data on either adults or juveniles during this period. It is known, however, that New York City was especially plagued by social problems because of an expanding and newly diverse population and a lack of social support. During the nineteenth century, it is estimated that thousands of children, perhaps between 5,000 and 30,000, lived on the streets. Some juveniles became involved in gangs, but most of their criminal behavior involved theft, not violence. In 1854, 80 percent of felony indictments and 50 percent of petty offenses for larceny were for juveniles under age 21. Despite the lack of violence in most crimes committed by juveniles, New York increasingly imposed harsh sentences on them. Before 1873, the New York justice system never sent more than six juveniles a year to prison, but in 1874 and 1876, 50 teenagers were sent to Sing Sing Prison. No specific provisions were made for juvenile offenders in most of the southern United States until after the war. Penitentiaries and prisons were almost empty at this time, as males were largely in the service. In contrast, reform schools were overfull, which was often attributed to increased delinquency due to absent fathers. Some reform schools even released older adolescents to military service, making more room for younger ones.[45]

CHILD-SAVING ACHIEVEMENTS

In 1853, Charles Loring Brace founded the New York Children's Aid Society. Brace acknowledged he was moved out of fear *of* children as much as from fear *for* children. Brace asserted, "There are no dangers to the property or the permanency of our institutions, so great as those from the existence of ... a class of vagabond, ignorant, or ungoverned children."[46] In addition, Brace coined the phrase "dangerous classes" to describe the "outcasts, vicious, reckless multitude of New York boys, swarming ... in every foul alley and low street."[47] Brace and other reformers felt that the western farm family was the model for character. Between 1855 and 1875, the Children's Aid Society sent an average of 3,000 children west each year.[48] Brace's "orphan trains" were responsible for moving more than 50,000 children from New York City.[49] Complaints that children were herded onto the orphan trains without their parents' permission surfaced as early as the 1870s. Midwestern states claimed that they were becoming dumping grounds for delinquents, and Catholics and Jews expressed concern that the trains were about converting children to Protestantism.[50] The last orphan train left New York in 1929. Importantly, the Children's Aid Society was one of the first institutions in America to use professional caseworkers instead of volunteers, to keep case records, and to conduct home visits, all hallmarks of later social workers.[51]

In the winter of 1873, a church worker in Hell's Kitchen, New York, named Etta Wheeler was informed about a case of child cruelty involving a young girl named Mary Ellen Wilson. At that time, there were no child protection laws or agencies to assist her, so Etta Wheeler decided she would use the next best thing—legislation prohibiting cruelty against animals. This successful attempt to remove Mary Ellen from her abusive parents led to the 1875 creation of the New York Society for the Prevention of Cruelty to Children (SPCC). In that same year, the New York state legislature authorized the establishment of branches of the organization in every county in the state.[52] Chapters quickly formed throughout the states, as reformers feared the disintegration of the family and the subsequent danger that their delinquent children would bring.[53] The SPCC was the first organization to recognize that children might need to enforce rights against their parents.[54] Over a decade later, similar laws and agencies were passed in the United Kingdom.[55] Other historians claim,

however, that there was some recognition in the previous century that children were treated poorly by parents and that at least some mechanisms were
in place to condemn and punish parents and to remove children.[56] Still others
contend that historians simply desire to represent the Progressive era and the
child savers as fundamentally different from those before them.[57]

Changes in school laws and practices were also on the Progressives agenda.
Schools were seen not just as educational institutions, but as an important
form of social control.[58] In 1852, Massachusetts passed the first compulsory
education law. By 1900, 32 states had compulsory education laws. Mississippi was the final state to add such a law in 1918.[59] School reformers applied
the features of scientific management, popular with the developing factories.
Teachers began to "specialize" in one grade, use a standardized curriculum,
and track students based on their ability.[60] Students were taught efficiency
and time management.[61] As compulsory education became more popular,
truancy became a greater problem. In 1862, Massachusetts adopted a law
allowing for the incarceration of chronic truants at reform schools. By the end
of the nineteenth century, policing of truants was built into the juvenile court
system.[62] Truancy laws were applied with some regularity. Of the children
jailed at Bridewell (Chicago House of Correction) in 1898, one-quarter were
there for truancy.[63] Echoing concerns about the basic nature of deviance,
the trend was to blame the parents. It was thought that truancy reflected
poor parenting and was a precursor to more serious delinquency. Yet only
two of the 178 children tracked for absence in 1906 were found to be truly
incorrigible. Poverty and ignorance of the family was the primary reason for
truancy.[64]

Progressives dealt with child labor laws as well. At the time, children
regularly labored in mines, furnace rooms, spinning rooms of cotton mills,
picking shrimp or shucking oysters, or canning fruit and vegetables. They
were exposed to all types of contaminants, adverse weather, and arduous conditions.[65] Poor families would frequently send a bright daughter or son to
work in a factory instead of to school, and orphaned and dependent children
were apprenticed to work in hazardous factories.[66] Although 28 states had
laws limiting child labor by 1900, the practice was still common.[67]

Child labor laws are generally seen as positive. However, "although protec-
tionist in intent, child labor laws also excluded youth from productive economic activity, denied them economic roles or self-sufficiency, isolated them
from adult work role models, and prolonged their financial dependence."[68]

One of the first, and the longest-lasting, innovations of the child savers was
the orphan asylum. Most inmates, however, were not truly orphans. In many
cases, single parents were unable to care for their children, or at least were

perceived by authorities as unable to do so.[69] By 1850, there were almost 100 of these orphanages.[70] This was part of a broader trend whereby reformers attempted to isolate, insulate, and control deviants.[71] Some orphan children ended up in prisons simply because they lived on the streets. For instance, in 1823, 450 children were incarcerated for this reason in New York's Bridewell and Newgate prisons.[72] In 1823, the New York City Society for the Prevention of Pauperism recommended the building of a House of Refuge, which would serve as an almshouse for vagrant children and a prison. The New York House of Refuge opened two years later. In its first four years, 527 children were admitted.[73]

EARLIEST PRISONS

New York's first penitentiary opened at Newgate in 1801. Newgate was championed by Quakers and was intended to offer a more rational form of punishment; instead, it was remembered as a hellhole for adult male offenders. As atrocities at Newgate became public, the New York state legislature authorized the building of a new penitentiary for adults in Auburn. The Auburn facility opened in 1817 with administrators taking a hard-line approach. They made liberal use of solitary confinement, despite the fact that New York had earlier rejected this form of penitence used in Pennsylvania. As in Pennsylvania, they soon remembered why—inmates were driven to insanity and solitary confinement diminished their resistance to disease. New York dismantled their solitary confinements in 1825.[74] These facility failures spawned numerous studies and reports and prompted an important ideological shift in corrections. Support grew for more rehabilitative programs, discipline, religion, and hard labor and less reliance on punishment and isolation.[75] Vengeance was no longer viewed as the way to deal with offenders; in fact, punishment based on revenge was seen as barbaric. Deterrence replaced vengeance as the primary reason to incarcerate.[76]

Additionally, major economic downturns in the early part of the nineteenth century forced many out of work. Unemployment, increasing numbers of Irish immigrants, and rapid industrialization all impacted the prevention and response to juvenile delinquency.[77]

HOUSES OF REFUGE

The New York House of Refuge opened in 1825 amidst these controversies. It was sponsored and managed by the same people involved in penal reform at the time. Managers often referred to the youth as "scholars" and compared the house with public schools. In reality, inmates spent only four hours per day in classrooms. Two hours involved moral indoctrination and two others were devoted to "mental improvement." In contrast, inmates spent eight hours in some form of labor.[78] Yet the managers struggled with precisely how to define their mission, comparing it at times with prisons, factories, workhouses, nurseries, hospitals, poor houses, and orphanages.[79] Managers boasted that the facility embodied the spirit of the Enlightenment, emphasizing reason and progress and the idea that the law could be used to change the human condition.[80]

Houses of refuge were a full-time residence for dependent, delinquent, and neglected youth. The initial population consisted of just six boys and three girls housed in an abandoned soldier's barracks. By the end of the year, however, the New York House held 69 inmates, 47 of which were admitted for stealing and vagrancy.[81]

Although the notion of the houses of refuge was popular with reformers, it wasn't until 1829 that public funds were allotted to pay operating costs. The movement to build houses of refuge spread rapidly, with Boston and Philadelphia opening facilities in 1826 and 1828, respectively. New Orleans was home to the first southern house, opened in 1847. By 1860, 16 houses of refuge had opened across the country.[82] A great concern was the housing of children with adult offenders, and houses of refuge allowed this separation.[83] As reformers also recognized that children will likely learn from their peers, they felt it even more essential that offenders be separated by the severity of their offenses.[84] The houses were undeniably designed to compel lower-class youth to conform to middle-class standards of behavior. Managers claimed the facility would, "reinforce the crumbling authority of impoverished parents over-burdened with the demands of daily life, giving them a potent symbol of fear with which to scare ungracious and disobedient children into humility and quiescence."[85]

Houses of refuge were similar to poorhouses of the era in two key ways. First, juveniles did not receive sentences adjusted for the severity of offense. Rather, boys were committed until their 21st birthday and girls until their 18th (later amended to 21 as well). Few were actually held that long, however. Commitment to the institution did not require a criminal conviction. A parent or a city alderman could admit a child.[86] Hence, while reformers claimed to be helping families, they were also diminishing the power of the family to make decisions about childrearing.

The houses of refuge were also lauded as a method to ensure that juvenile offenders were indeed punished. Like today, there was great concern that juveniles were released too easily, and that sympathetic juries failed to convict obviously guilty youth.[87] Reformers who started the houses were concerned with the horrible condition of local jails, where juveniles were often housed with adults. They were also concerned that judges and juries were acquitting clearly responsible juveniles because they did not want them committed to these facilities.[88]

Managers claimed to have replaced inhumane methods of discipline, such as beatings and whippings, with more persuasive methods. They asserted that all children could learn appropriate behavior if instructors tapped into their curiosity and reason.[89] The house was also described as a mini-democracy, stressing character, merit, and willingness to help others. Like modern-day prison rewards for good behavior, inmates were given "badges of distinction" when they performed chores without complaint and demonstrated the "right attitude." It was also alleged that there would be no stigma associated with their imprisonment. In fact, their work and education at the house was said to better prepare youth to live in the modern world.[90] "Education in this emerging juvenile justice system fit as part of the greater plan of the reformers, society, and judges. They considered education for all to be a collective remedy for delinquents and others of this temperament."[91]

Refuges received referrals from those who administered programs for the poor, from constables, from parents, and from schools.[92] Because there was no distinction in the eyes of reformers between criminal and noncriminal behavior—both were seen as the effect of defective social environment—reformers claimed their proceedings were civil, not criminal.[93]

Houses of refuge generally followed strict gender and racial segregation protocols. Sexual immorality was seen as a primary reason for institutionalizing girls.[94] The early houses either excluded blacks completely or housed them in a separate location. The first House of Refuge for Colored Juvenile Delinquents was opened in Philadelphia in 1849.[95]

In reality, the houses fell far short of the claims made by child savers. The daily routine for incarcerated youth was similar to the prisons at Auburn and Sing Sing in the emphasis on order, obedience, and work. Rather than preparing youth for middle-class success upon release, the facility emphasized submission. Even the architecture of the facility looked more like a penitentiary than a school. Within a few years of opening, the managers had erected a tall surrounding wall and several stone buildings with individual cells that were intended for solitary confinement.[96]

Although they invoked religion to justify their actions, the primary concern for many of these reformers was to retain their class privileges. Many have called the founders of the houses "Conservative Reformers," as they were typically affluent males who viewed themselves as "God's elect."[97] As

Criminologists Krisberg and Austin explained, "The philanthropy of this group was aimed at reestablishing the social order, while preserving the existing property and status relationships."[98]

In the early days, houses of refuge in New York and Philadelphia were widely heralded for treating inmates with humanity, for their quality academic instruction and for their reported rates of rehabilitated inmates, remarkably (and unbelievably) between 75 and 95 percent. By the mid-nineteenth century it became clear that the houses of refuge were not succeeding in rehabilitating youth. Greater scrutiny of daily life inside the houses contradicted the claims of humane treatment and educational achievement. Whippings with the cat or rattan, applied to the palm, the back of the hands, the tops and bottom of feet, and to both the clothed and naked buttocks were used, according to an assistant superintendent, "everywhere at all times of the day."[99] Inmates were frequently whipped or placed in solitary for failure to follow the daily schedule; some were even punished for slow labor.[100] One estimate was that up to 40 percent of children held in houses of refuge escaped from them or from their apprenticeship. One thing the houses did do was to produce income; the income coming from labor sold to outside contractors covered approximately 40 percent of the operating costs for the facilities.[101] Although many of the inmates had never been tried for any specific criminal act, managers made it clear that they treated all of them as guilty offenders.[102]

Overcrowding became a serious issue in the houses of refuge. One popular method to alleviate crowded conditions was called "placing out." Placing out involved the transfer of inmates to more rural locales, sometimes within the state or to newly opened facilities in the Midwest, under the premise that urban areas were more criminogenic. After being observed working in these locations, inmates were then indentured into service until the age of 21. Approximately 90 percent of the releases from houses of refuge came from these indentured relationships.[103] In addition to the above failures, corruption was rampant, Catholic proselytizing occurred despite the wishes of families, serious offenders mingled regularly with lesser and even innocent offenders, sexual exploitation was not uncommon, many inmates showed significant emotional problems, and youth were exploited for their cheap labor but learned few useful vocational skills.[104]

One historian explained why the refuges failed. "In the search for order, they veered too far to the side of egregious discipline and punishment and soon became nothing more than warehouses for troublesome children. Yet even in their failure they succeeded in establishing incarceration as the response of choice to all types of juvenile deviance, long after the goal of 'moral education' had ceased to be taken seriously."[105] In essence, the refuges helped normalize state involvement for a number of diverse offenses, and make detention of some sort the common sense response. "In exchange for receiving a new and quite punitive 'father,' juveniles gave up their traditional rights under criminal law. Commitment to the refuge meant that vagrancy and 'trifling offenses' could be dealt with the same as more serious offenses since they could be viewed as signs of 'vicious propensities' [of the child]."[106] The following is a summary of the major changes emerging from the houses of refuge: "Refuge legislation embodied three legal innovations: a formal age-based distinction between juvenile and adult offenders and their institutional separation, the use of indeterminate commitments, and a broadened legal authority that encompassed both criminal offenders and neglected and incorrigible children."[107]

Reform Schools

A more aggressive approach to youth problems emerged in 1895, when philanthropist William R. George started the George Youth Republic in Freeville, New York, as a refuge for delinquent or potentially delinquent youth. Like Charles Loring Brace, George felt that city life was the root of many social ills. Rather than the republican enclave committed to self-government George claimed it to be, George's refuge was mired in claims of brutality and sexual abuse. Still, some 3,000 boys and girls lived there.[108]

In the middle of the nineteenth century, a new alternative to the reformatory appeared. Championed as being better suited to rehabilitate delinquents without relying on force or the threat of force, cottage or family reform schools were adopted in Massachusetts, Ohio, Wisconsin, Illinois (Chicago, specifically), and Indiana. Although reformatories of all types were often referred to using domestic metaphors like homes, cottages, and families, only the ones in these states differed from the average penal-inspired facility.[109]

Reformers of the period were heavily influenced by European ways of dealing with delinquent and wayward youth. Two family reform schools served as the primary models for American reformers: Johann Wichern's Rauhe Haus near Hamburg, Germany, and Frederic DeMetz's Colonie Agricole in Mettray, France. Although some educational reformers, most notably, Horace Mann, were well aware of these models for several decades, two child welfare conventions in New York City in 1857 and 1859 brought them to the attention of juvenile justice reformers. Although there were defenders of the houses of refuge at the conventions, the prevailing sentiment was one of critique. Family reform school advocates maintained that they were able to introduce greater personal contact into the daily routine, which was much needed for rehabilitation. Recognizing children's need to be loved and to love, the family reform houses stressed the frequency and quality of human interactions rather than a specified content.[110] Between one and three dozen inmates with similar personality traits were housed in small homes or cottages under the supervision of a surrogate mother or father. These "families" lived, worked, and attended school together. Interaction with other inmates was infrequent. This was in stark contrast to the cells or barracks-like dorms used in the houses, and to their uniform schedule, mingling of all types of inmates, and lack of close authority figures. The idea was that children would learn respect and good habits from the surrogate family.[111]

Massachusetts opened the nation's first state-sponsored reformatory in 1848. Maine established a reformatory in 1853, Connecticut in 1854, and Ohio in 1858.[112] Reformatories differed significantly from one another, but all followed several main principles: that young offenders be separated from adult offenders; that delinquents must be removed from their environment "for their own good"; that delinquents could be committed without trial; that sentences were to be indeterminate; that inmates not be idle nor indulgent; that reformatories work best when located in the country; that labor, education, and religion were key to reform; and that inmates must be taught sobriety, industry, thrift, ambition, and prudence.[113]

Unlike houses of refuge, reformatories were state-supported from the outset. Built like a penitentiary, reformatories were intended never to house more than 300 inmates. Within a few years, however, the reformatory was filled to capacity. To avoid overcrowding, an addition that doubled the capacity was erected. This, too, was soon full.[114]

In 1854, the state legislature voted to open the first institution for female delinquents. Based on the notion that females' physical and emotional make-up was more delicate than males', the facility was modeled after the family reform schools in Europe. Girls lived in houses of 30 with a matron and an assistant. Houses were designed to look as much like an average middle-class family home as possible. Allegedly, the houses would make delinquent and wayward girls feel as though someone cared about them. The goal, according to trustees, was, "to educate, to teach them industry, self-reliance, morality and religion, and prepare them to go forth qualified to become useful and respectful members of society. All this is to be done, without stone walls, bars or bolts, but by the more sure and effective restraining power—*the cords of love.*"[115]

The nation's first family reform school attracted national attention. Around the same time, the Massachusetts State Reform School caught fire, destroying almost half of the facility. Reconstruction was approved that modeled the female facility.[116] Another factor encouraging use of the 1850s family reform model was the increasing concern over any form of long-term institutional care. The impact of evangelical Christians is evident, as they asserted long-term institutionalization did not change convictions, it merely elicited compliant behavior.

The shifts in childrearing philosophy described earlier contributed to the challenges to houses of refuge and reformatories. New philosophies for nurturing children were printed in many books and widely circulated newspapers. Adolescence was beginning to be viewed as a separate and distinct developmental phase, following the work of G. Stanley Hall (discussed earlier in the chapter). Reformers held on to earlier Calvinist ideology, still stressing obedience, yet began to replace "spare the rod" approaches with more persuasive and affectionate approaches. This was also true in schools, where corporal punishment declined dramatically.[117]

While reformers paid much lip service to the educational mission of reformatories, in reality, the schooling offered nothing more than teaching the poor and deviant to accept their lot.[118] In 1891, Homer Folks, President of the Pennsylvania Children's Aid Society, described five major problems with reform schools. These included the temptation for parents and guardians to absolve themselves of responsibility, the negative influence of association with delinquent peers, the stigma of having been committed, the lack of individualization, and the failure of reform schools to simulate and prepare their charges for life in the real world.[119] By 1910, the reformatory experiment ended, leaving the legacy of the indeterminate sentence, conditional release, educational programs, vocational training, and rehabilitation in general.[120]

CHILD-SAVING ORGANIZATIONS

Chicago was the site of a number of different reform movements in the later 1800s. The Charity Organization Society (COS), started in 1883, attempted to organize the city's charity workers. In addition, the COS stressed that the poor be treated with kindness and sympathy. They did, however, distinguish between "worthy" and "unworthy" poor. Wounded veterans and newly widowed mothers, for instance, were worthy of aid, while the "immoral, inebriate, and feebleminded" did not deserve assistance.[121] The other critical effort in Chicago was the settlement house movement. The idea of the settlement house came from London in 1884, when vicar Samuel A. Barnett, his wife, and some university students took residence in a poor part of the city to help the impoverished. In contrast to the COS, settlement house workers lived in the poor neighborhoods. Rather than emphasizing charity, the settlement houses were intended as a way to mix social classes and to show the wealthy how the poor really lived. Thus, settlement houses were an attempt to eschew the elitism of the COS and other reform organizations. Settlement house workers were also more prone to emphasize poverty as an environmental concern, rather than a hereditary condition.[122] "While some historians view the settlers' actions simply as attempts to impose middle-class values on the lower classes, others offer a more nuanced view of the settlers' moral outlook. Some lower-class women wanted nurses and others to help them in parenting skills and other life adjustments."[123]

From 1885 on, a number of social agencies, such as the Boy's Club, the Young Men's Christian Association (YMCA), and the Young Women's Christian Association (YWCA), emerged from Christian benevolence. They also came from concerns about the maintenance of social class positions.[124] In 1887, Lucy Flower and the Chicago Women's Club helped create the Protective Agency for Women and Children. The Agency provided legal assistance, housing, and employment to women and girls who had been swindled, violently beaten by fathers or guardians, or sexually assaulted. This effort was in stark contrast to the predominant view that women and girls were carriers of disease, temptation, and immorality.[125] The Industrial School for Girls was also established in this time period, and housed girls aged 10–16 who were begging, loitering in houses of ill fame, wandering streets or alleys, consorting with thieves, or living in poorhouses. Delinquent girls were committed to the Geneva Reformatory for Girls, created in 1895. Girls were subjected to mandatory pelvic examinations and vaginal cultures in order to see if they had engaged in sexual activity and to gather information about sexually transmitted diseases.[126]

In 1889, Jane Addams established Hull House, a settlement house largely for poor immigrants. Addams maintained that settlement house workers must be open and tolerant to cultural and behavioral differences.[127] The beginning of the twentieth century also saw the development of the term "social services" to describe methods and techniques designed to improve the lot of the urban poor.

Conditions in rapidly changing Chicago worried the progressives, who maintained that social problems were generally due to the environment and could, consequently, be changed.[128]

Chicago in the late nineteenth century presented a series of stark contrasts. While Potter Palmer's mansion contained a seventy-five-foot-long art gallery filled with rare French Impressionist paintings, 74 percent of the city's population lived in buildings without a bathroom. While George M. Pullman spent thirty-eight thousand dollars on a specially built railroad "palace" car to transport him between his three manor houses, tenement dwellers in Chicago earned about sixteen cents an hour during sixty-hour workweeks. And, while the children of the well-to-do young ladies like Katherine Dummer or young gentleman like Henry Black Fuller, finished their schooling before setting off on a grand tour of Europe, lower-class youths were arrested for stealing pipes to sell to the junkman and sent to a crowded jail cell in which they were housed with hardened criminals.[129]

Chicago's population expanded to five times its size between 1870 and 1900. Much of this was due to immigration. By 1900, the foreign-born population was larger than the entire city had been just 18 years prior.[130] Poor areas of the city were densely populated. One 1901 estimate placed 45,643 people in less than one-third of a square mile. This type of crowding, coupled with the lack of indoor plumbing in most homes, poor drainage and sewage, and malnutrition, was a breeding ground for disease and death. Yet, most of the affluent of Chicago were largely unaware of the misery in the poor districts of the city, as they spent no time outside their own social circles.[131]

In sum, the Chicago Progressives focused on two strategies, often combined: helping the poor by making them assimilate, and helping the poor by advocating social changes.[132] Many Progressives called upon the gospel, seeing the betterment of society as their Christian mission. Another driving force was what some called "urban housekeeping." This approach centered on women's special role as mothers, seeing the city as a macro-scale family of which the mother was to care. Many of the most vocal and effective Progressives were women, in particular in regard to the formation of the juvenile courts. Reform organizations were very appealing to the educated middle-class women, who had learned about social concerns in their courses but found few job opportunities available to them.[133]

Progressive era ideas naturally had the most impact on middle-class families. Because of economic changes, middle-class families had limited their size, thus allowing them to invest more, both financially and emotionally, in the rearing of their children.[134] The reformers were hardly saintly; most were terribly prejudiced against immigrants, as was most of the population. The Spanish-American War in 1898 was a visible symbol of American empire, and these reformers, while recognizing the need for immigrants, felt they needed to assimilate as quickly as possible.[135]

A variety of rationales were used for the greater involvement of government.

Some spoke in Christian terms, emphasizing brotherhood under Christ or the state's soul-saving possibilities. Others expressed these ideas in secular terms, describing society as an organic whole in which everyone is responsible for everyone else. Some viewed the state as parent, with duties to care for her children. And all expected that enhancing the state's responsibilities would serve practical ends, such as reducing public expenditures on relief. Expanding the state's powers was necessary to save the children, according to some reformers, even if that meant taking children away from their parents.[136]

Some reformers, however, struggled with precisely how much intervention was appropriate and in which cases it should occur. Judge Orrin N. Carter, a judge in Cook County and an 18-year justice on the Supreme Court of Illinois, expressed in 1901, "It is very difficult to say when we ought to interfere with the home and when we ought not to … I have read papers very recently by most excellent people who think this question of State supervision is very easy of solution, but you must remember that we have all sorts of people and all sorts of families; that the home life is the very foundation of our present civilization, and that all that is sweet and ennobling in this country has started from the home."[137] Others felt no such caution was warranted. Lucy Flower, a well-to-do reformer involved in many different efforts, expressed, "To my mind it presents no difficulty, for I believe the good of the child and the right of the State to control its citizenship are superior to any claim of the parent who is unfit or who willfully fails to perform his duty to his child."[138]

One of the most significant achievements of Progressive reformers was the development of an informal probation system, which became codified in the Juvenile Court Law of 1899. From December 1897 on, a Dr. Moore met with parents at the home, working as a liaison between them and the police.[139] The most common form of action by any social service agency in the 1900s was removal of the child.[140] Some have maintained that, while reformers were certainly concerned about the welfare of children, their real concern was that neglected and abused children had become an eyesore, arguing "'seeing' the poor was regarded as equivalent to 'knowing' them."[141] Seeing these children bothered the middle-class reformers, who felt children belonged in the home. They referred to neglected and abused children as, "arabs, urchins, guttersnipes, as a wild race, nomadic, a multitude of untutored savages."[142] In essence, reform was conceptualized as a means of control. In addition to the new visibility of street children, the duties of social workers changed such that they were charged with seeing the inside of children's homes. While some social workers had always expressed fear and disgust, descriptions became more vivid. The following is a report from an inspector who feared contamination from his home visit: "When I got home I had caught 26 fleas. I had to have a bath and change all my clothing. I even had a flea in my hair. I did no see any other class of vermin on the children." Another wrote, "The smell of the house is so disgusting that I am compelled to smoke to keep the taste out of my mouth."[143]

JUVENILES AND THE COURT SYSTEM, PRE-1900

Parens patriae was established as precedent in the states by the 1838 *Ex Parte* Crouse case, when Mary Ann Crouse was committed to the Philadelphia House of Refuge. Crouse's mother had her committed for "vicious conduct" without the knowledge of her father.[144] The court rejected her father's assertion that Mary Ann's incarceration without a jury trial was a violation of the Sixth Amendment.[145] Two key themes that impacted correctional literature until the start of the twentieth century emerged from the case. First, that the government can interfere with the natural dealings of a family and incarcerate children in order to *prevent* delinquency. Second, that houses of refuge were essentially no different than public schools.[146] Regarding the former, the court adhered to a concept of community that was rapidly eroding. They held that the community had an important interest in the "proper socialization" of a child. The attitude is perhaps best summed up by educational reformer John Dewey, who said, "What the best and wisest parent wants for his own child, that must the community want for all its children."[147] In the event that parents were incompetent to socialize that child, the courts had little choice but to remand the child into other custody—much like the modern-day mantra, "It takes a village." Once a child was removed from his or her "incapable" parents and incarcerated in a reformatory, it was quite difficult for the parents to convince the courts they were actually able.[148] To assume that there is a consensus on "proper socialization" was presumptuous, given the demographic shifts, securalization, and commercial developments of the time.[149] Yet again, these decisions reflect the elitism of the reformers.

Slave children were generally not offered the protections of *parens patriae.* Thus, social welfare institutions generally ignored black children and, at the same time, limited assistance to white children "could be rationalized by the notion that they were treated better than Black slaves."[150] The elitism of the courts is also clear from their rationale. In the Crouse case, it was argued that Mary Ann "had been snatched from a course which must have ended in conformed depravity: and not only is the restraint of her person lawful, but it would have been an act of extreme cruelty to release her from it."[151]

Regarding the second important theme, the Crouse decision authenticated for many the claims that reformatories were educational institutions with the goals of teaching children morality, work skills, and, at the same time, to isolate them from corrupt influences. Reformatories were not, according to these judges, punitive in nature, but were schools for reformation, and to be confined in one was no more burdensome than is required at every school.[152] "As to the abridgement of indefeasible rights by confinement of the person, it is no more than what is borne, to a greater or less extent, in every school;

and we know of no natural right to exemption from restraints which conduce to an infant's welfare."[153] Court after court reified the comparison between reformatories and schools. In doing so, they failed to investigate the actual conditions in the reformatories or to question whether they were achieving all that they claimed.[154]

Not until 1870 did a state court handle a challenge to these two premises. Daniel O' Connell was assigned an indefinite term at the Chicago Reform School for violating an 1867 statute. The statute provided for the apprehension of boys and girls between the ages of six and 16 who were vagrant, destitute or lacking proper parental care, or who were "growing up in mendicancy, ignorance, idleness or vice."[155] *People v. Turner* challenged Crouse in four key ways. First, the judges questioned the analogy between public schools and reformatories, arguing that imprisonment, by nature, is punitive. Second, *Turner* demonstrated concern that "proper parenting" was too narrowly defined and advocated broader consideration of childrearing styles. Third, the court affirmed that parental rights should not be abrogated except when the strongest reasons were present, saying, "Parenthood emanated from God, and every attempt to infringe upon it, except from dire necessity, should be resisted in all well governed States."[156] Fourth, the *Turner* court held that children have inviolable rights, even the children of the poor who were typically the beneficiaries of the state's "benevolence." Although *Turner* issued a broad challenge to the dominance of the parental state approach, it did not last for long. The appellate courts overturned *Turner,* and, in doing so, restated the two key ideas from Crouse.

Child-saving organizations saw the initial decision as irresponsible and denounced it as setting back their important mission of intervening with delinquent youth.[157] In another critical decision affirming *parens patriae, Milwaukee Industrial School v. Supervisors of Milwaukee County,* the Wisconsin Supreme Court delineated the conditions for which children and youth could be committed to the local industrial school. These "offenses," more like pre-offenses, were widely adopted into later juvenile codes. They included begging; offering anything for sale in public; being found wandering; being found destitute, as an orphan, or having imprisoned parents; frequenting the company of thieves, lewd, wanton, or lascivious persons; being an inmate of a poorhouse or house of ill fame; or simply being without subsistence or support.[158] Referring to *parens patriae,* one prominent educator wrote, "The doctrine rests on one reasonable assumption: children are members of society, and society as a whole benefits from the contributions and suffers from the difficulties of each child. But it opens, as well, the possibility of all kinds of abuse, beginning with the Crown exercising power in an abusive or arbitrary manner."[159]

THE DEVELOPMENT OF THE JUVENILE COURT SYSTEM

Women were integral in establishing the Juvenile Court, yet these influential women knew that the legislation must be set forward by men. Illinois women did not have the right to vote at the turn of the century. Private clubs, often women's clubs, generally started reform efforts with little or no budget and using volunteers, thereby making them indispensable before they were set forward for school board or legislative consideration. The Chicago Women's Club (CWC) used this strategy to establish kindergartens and to pass a compulsory education law.[160] In 1866, Adelaide B. Groves, a former teacher, visited the Chicago House of Correction. She was appalled at seeing small boys housed with murderers and other hardened criminals, and immediately reported her dismay to the CWC as well as to the superintendent of the institution. When he told her there was no room to separate the boys from the others, she used her teaching skills to begin reading to and instructing the boys. She and another teacher appealed to the CWC, and the organization raised funds to support a teacher for the boys. The teacher, Florence Hayburn, also asked Judge Richard S. Tuthill to hear the boys' cases ahead of the others on the docket, which he did by hearing them on Saturdays. In 1897, the state took over the salary for the teacher.[161] The CWC also worked to educate the public about issues related to children and women.

The actual juvenile court bill was introduced on February 7, 1899. The Senate eliminated several of its' provisions, including one ensuring that the state pay for establishing and maintaining the court. Another section prohibited the court from compensating probation officers. The *Chicago Tribune* endorsed the juvenile court bill, arguing it would relieve police of many duties they currently held involving children, it would take children away from prisons where they were schooled in crime, it would not brand children as "criminals," and it was simply long overdue.[162]

The primary opposition to the bill came from men involved with industrial schools and reformatories. They feared reduced revenues if fewer young people were sent their way. Some police also resisted, as they felt the court system might threaten the discretion they held when dealing with youth.[163] Opposition efforts were never highly organized, and the bill moved relatively easily through the legislature. The final bill had 21 sections detailing the court's jurisdiction and processes. A 1905 amendment provided for judges to appoint probation officers and authorized their pay by the Board of County commissioners, although the funding did not appear until 1908.[164]

One historian has maintained, "the juvenile court was distinctive in terms of its institutional character and administrative ideology" and that it was "readily accepted because it was an exemplar of the least controversial and most broadly legitimate aspects of a general Progressive reform agenda and, more specifically, of the movement for charity organization."[165] In essence, the court helped institute an ideology of control of "stubborn children" in a formal way. "The major accomplishment of the juvenile court was administrative, in that it provided a legally sanctioned arena within which diagnostic investigations could be conducted and therapeutic treatment initiated."[166]

In some locations, the idea of child welfare legislation like that of the juvenile court laws was already well developed. For instance, Massachusetts defeated a 1905 bill providing for one judge to hear all children's cases because it was not radical enough.[167] "In short, the court could accommodate a broad base of support precisely because little about it was controversial."[168] There is still some dispute over the first state to provide for special proceedings for young people. Although Illinois was the first to formally enact one, Massachusetts and New York, in 1874 and 1892, respectively, provided for separate trials, and Colorado is said to have had a working juvenile court in 1899, under famous Judge Ben Lindsey.[169]

In conclusion, child savers operated from a fear *for* perspective. They generally felt their actions were required to save children, without considering that their benevolence was not always so beneficial.

NOTES

1. Degler, C. (1980). *At odds: Women and the family in America from the revolution to the present.* New York: Oxford University Press.

2. Krisberg, B. & Austin, J. (1993). *Reinventing juvenile justice.* Newbury Park, CA: Sage.

3. Platt, A. (1998). The child-saving movement and the origins of the juvenile justice system. In P. Sharp & B. Hancock (Eds.). *Juvenile delinquency: Historical, theoretical, and societal reactions to youth* (2nd ed.) (pp. 3–17). Upper Saddle River, NJ: Prentice Hall.

4. Ibid.

5. Feld, B. (1999). *Bad kids: Race and the transformation of the juvenile court.* New York: Oxford University Press.

6. Krisberg & Austin (1993).

7. Feld (1999).

8. Polier, J. (1989). Juvenile justice in double jeopardy: The distanced community and vengeful retribution. Hillsdale, NJ: Lawrence Erlbaum Associates, pp. 1–2.

9. Platt (1998), p. 36.

10. Mintz, S. (2004). *Huck's raft: A history of American childhood.* Cambridge, MA: The Belknap Press of Harvard University Press, p. 155.

11. Sutton, J. (1988). *Stubborn children.* Berkeley, CA: University of California Press.

12. Feld (1999).

13. Getis, V. (2000). *The juvenile court & the progressives.* Urbana, IL: University of Illinois Press, p. 21.

14. Grossberg, M. (2002). Changing conceptions of child welfare in the United States, 1820–1935. In M. Rosenheim, F. Zimring, D. Tanenhaus, & B. Dohrn (Eds.) *A century of juvenile justice* (pp. 3–41). Chicago, IL: The University of Chicago Press.

15. Watkins, J. (1998). *The juvenile justice century.* Durham, NC: Carolina Academic Press.

16. Feld (1999).

17. Sutton (1988), p. 145.

18. Feld (1999).

19. Getis (2000).

20. Feld (1999), pp. 52–53.

21. Rothman, D. (1980). *Conscience and convenience: The asylum and its alternative in Progressive America.* Boston, MA: Little, Brown, and Co., p. 60.

22. Sutton (1888), pp. 49–50.

23. Platt (1998).

24. Holmes, S., & Holmes, R. (2002). *Sex crimes* (2nd ed.). Thousand Oaks, CA: Sage.

25. Schmalleger, F. (2005). *Criminology today* (3rd ed.). Upper Saddle River, NJ: Prentice Hall.

26. Ibid.

27. Platt (1998), p. 8.

28. Schmalleger (2005).

29. Scott, E. (2002). The legal construction of childhood. In M. Rosenheim, F. Zimring, D. Tanenhaus, & B. Dohrn (Eds.). *A century of juvenile justice* (pp. 113–141). Chicago, IL: The University of Chicago Press.

30. Feld (1999).

31. Ibid.

32. Ibid.

33. Schmalleger (2005).

34. Getis (2000), p. 18.

35. Ibid.

36. Cited in Platt (1998), p. 10.

37. Mintz (2004).

38. Ibid., p. 191.

39. Ibid.

40. Ibid., p. 120.

41. Ibid.

42. Ibid.

43. Ibid.

44. Ibid., p. 154.

45. Vito, G. & Simonsen, C. (2004). *Juvenile justice today* (4th ed.). Upper Saddle River, NJ: Prentice Hall.

46. Cited in Bremner, R. (1970). *Children and Youth in America, Vol. One.* Cambridge, MA: Harvard University Press, p. 757.

47. Brace, C. (1872). *The Dangerous classes of New York and Twenty Years work among them.* New York: Wynkoop and Hallenbeck, p. 28–29.

48. Schlossman, S. (1977). *Love and the American delinquent.* Chicago, IL: University of Chicago Press.

49. Grossberg (2002).

50. Mintz (2004).

51. Ibid.

52. Ferguson, H. (2004). *Protecting children in our time; Child abuse, child protection and* The consequences of modernity. New York: Palgrave MacMillan.

53. Grossberg (2002).

54. Ibid.

55. Ferguson (2004).

56. Pollock, L. (1983). *Forgotten children: parent-child relations from 1500–1900.* Cambridge, MA: Cambridge University Press.

57. Ibid.

58. Feld (1999).

59. Edelman, P. (2002). American government and the politics of youth. In M. Rosenheim, F. Zimring, D. Tanenhaus, & B. Dohrn (Eds.). *A century of juvenile justice* (pp. 310–340). Chicago, IL: The University of Chicago Press.

60. Feld (1999).

61. Postman, N. (1994). *The disappearance of childhood.* New York: Vintage.

62. Feld (1999).

63. Dohrn, B. (2002). The school, the child, and the court. In M. Rosenheim, F. Zimring, D. Tanenhaus, & B. Dohrn (Eds.). *A century of juvenile justice* (pp. 267–309). Chicago, IL: The University of Chicago Press.

64. Ibid.

65. Trattner, W. (1970). Crusade for the children: A history of the National Child Labor Committee and child labor reform in New York state. Chicago, IL: Quadrangle.

66. Dohrn (2002).

67. Edelman (2002).

68. Feld (1999), p. 43.

69. Mintz (2004).

70. Ibid.

71. Katz, M. (1986). *In the shadow of the poorhouse: A social history of welfare in America.* New York: Basic.

72. Mintz (2004).

73. Ibid.

74. Schlossman (1977).

75. Ibid.

76. Ibid.

77. Krisberg & Austin (1993).

78. Schlossman (1977).

79. Ibid.

80. Ibid.

81. Watkins (1998).

82. Ibid.

83. Schlossman (1977).

84. Ibid.

85. Ibid., p. 24.

86. Watkins (1998).

87. Schlossman (1977).

88. Krisberg & Austin (1993).

89. Schlossman (1977).

90. Ibid.

91. Keeley, J. (2004, December). The metamorphosis of juvenile correctional education: Incidental conception to intentional conclusion. *The Journal of Correctional Education, 55*(4) 277–29, 284–85.

92. Feld (1999).

93. Ibid.

94. Grossberg (2002).

95. Krisberg & Austin (1993).

96. Schlossman (1977).

97. Krisberg & Austin (1993), p. 16.

98. Ibid., p. 16.

99. Schlossman (1977), p. 35.

100. Ibid.

101. Krisberg & Austin (1993).

102. Schlossman (1977).

103. Watkins (1998).

104. Schlossman (1977).

105. Sutton (1988), p. 47.

106. Lerman, P. (1991). Delinquency and social policy: A historical perspective. In E. Monkkonen (Ed.). *Crime & justice in American history: Delinquency and disorderly behavior* (pp. 23–33). Westport, CT: Meckler Publishing, p. 28.

107. Feld (1999), p. 151.

108. Mintz (2004).

109. Schlossman (1977).

110. Ibid.

111. Ibid.

112. Watkins (1998).

113. Platt, A. (1977). *The Child Savers: The invention of delinquency* (2nd ed.). Chicago, IL: University of Chicago Press.

114. Watkins (1998).

115. Schlossman (1977), p. 41.

116. Ibid.

117. Ibid.

118. Platt (1977).

119. Mennel, R. (1973). *Thorns and thistles.* Hanover: University of New Hampshire Press.

120. Inciardi, J. (1996). *Criminal Justice* (5th ed.). New York: Harcourt Brace.

121. Getis (2000), p. 15.

122. Ibid.

123. Ibid., p. 16.

124. Platt (1979).

125. Dohrn (2002).

126. Ibid.

127. Watkins (1998).

128. Getis (2000).

129. Ibid., p. 9.

130. Ibid.

131. Ibid.

132. Ibid.

133. Ibid.

134. Clapp, E. (1995, March 17). The Chicago Juvenile Court movement in the 1890s. Retrieved March 19, 2006 from: www.le.ac.uk/hi/teaching/papers/clapp1.html.

135. Getis (2000).

136. Ibid., p. 23.

137. Ibid., p. 25.

138. Ibid., p. 25.

139. Clapp (1995).

140. Ferguson (2004).

141. Ibid., p. 29.

142. Ibid., p. 35.

143. Ibid., p. 65.

144. Watkins (1998).

145. Schlossman (1977).

146. Ibid.

147. Dewey, J. (1899). *The school and society.* Chicago, IL: University of Chicago press, p. 3.

148. Watkins (1998).

149. Schlossman (1977).

150. Billingsley, A., & Giovannoni, J. (1972). *Children of the storm: Black children and American child welfare.* New York: Twyne Publishers, pp. 23–24.

151. Schlossman (1977), p.9.

152. Watkins (1998).

153. Schlossman (1977), p. 11.

154. Watkins (1998).

155. Schlossman (1977), p. 11.

156. Ibid., p. 12.

157. Platt (1977).

158. Watkins (1998).

159. Ayers, W. (1998). *A kind and just parent*. New York: Beacon, p. 43.

160. Getis (2000).

161. Ibid.

162. Ibid.

163. Wolcott, D. (2001, Winter). "The cop will get you": The police and discretionary juvenile justice, 1890–1940. *Journal of Social History*. Retrieved March 19, 2006 from: www.looksmarttrends.com/p/articles/mi_m2005/is_2_35/ai?8206 6734?pi=dyn.

164. Getis (2000).

165. Sutton (1988), p. 123.

166. Ibid., p. 149.

167. Ibid.

168. Ibid., p. 181.

169. Platt (1998).

3

Late Progressive Era

The early twentieth century was a pivotal time in juvenile justice. Debates about ambiguities in the juvenile justice system are some of the same that exist today. In addition, the attitude toward juvenile offenders and the philosophy of the fledgling courts shaped current attitudes and court structures.

Reform activities continued at the turn of the century. In 1909, President Theodore Roosevelt invited a number of social service professionals to the White House Conference on the Care of Dependent Children, the first national effort to promote a social services agenda. Their primary determination was that the federal government should establish a national agency devoted to children. In 1912, the Children's Bureau was created for this purpose. In 1920, the Child Welfare League of America was founded with a similar mission.[1] The Children's Bureau was authorized to report on all matters dealing with child welfare, including infant mortality and birth rate, occupations, accidents, and diseases of children, as well as matters dealing with the juvenile courts.[2] The Bureau's first leader was Julia Lathrop, who later joined philanthropist Julia Flower in the quest to establish a juvenile court.[3] Fear for the autonomy of families lead to a provision prohibiting Children's Bureau agents from entering a home without permission.[4] At the same time, the elitism of reformers was clear in that they continued to dictate what was best for other people's children. Reform activities significantly lessened after World War I. Many Americans were skeptical of the pacifism of reformers like Jane Addams, and funding was diverted to other sources.[5]

Because soldiers needed to be physically fit, the 1910s saw a big surge in programs promoting physical fitness for young men. In addition, there was great concern that, with fathers absent due to war, boys without a father figure would be emasculated. With the absence of many fathers, even more attention was given to mothers as the source of their children's delinquency. In some cases, reform institutions accepted aggression from boys because it demonstrated they were not emasculated.[6]

World War I also impacted the approach to juvenile corrections, beginning with titles and names. Living units were called barracks, kids wore uniforms, and the staff were called captains, majors, and colonels.[7] Others documented the increased focus on Americanization and citizenship skills in the Chicago Home for Girls as well.[8]

The war also generated anti-immigrant sentiments. As will be discussed, the new juvenile courts were already prone to blame and target poor immigrant families. This was only exacerbated by the war.[9]

Shortly after the start of the Chicago court, other states enacted juvenile court legislation. In 1902, Milwaukee, Buffalo, and New York City added juvenile courts, and in 1903, 19 other cities had them.[10] By 1927, all states except Maine and Wyoming had enacted legislation authorizing a juvenile court, with these two states doing so shortly after World War II. By 1932, there were more than 600 juvenile courts throughout the United States. Within a generation, most major Western nations had some form of juvenile court inspired by the U.S. example.[11] The courts varied in organization, with some being established as a special branch or session of another court, such as a district court, others created as free-standing, independent courts, and still others defined by a specific geographic region, such as a county court.[12]

The competing attitudes of fear for children and fear of children were evident in the early twentieth century.[13] Many lauded the new juvenile justice system as a dramatic improvement with delinquent youth and praised the Progressives for their concern about humanity. Others were more critical. In reference to Progressive era changes, one author has argued, "the well-meaning intent of reform has turned into the tyranny of reform; the state now has gained greater social control over the dependent youngster."[14] Some have maintained that the real goal of the court reformers was diversionary, not interventionist. The interventionist goal is the one that received the bulk of attention, as it was profoundly new. This goal was that the court, as well as other social services, should be actively involved in intervening in the lives of at-risk youth. In contrast, the diversionary goal was simply to avoid the harms associated with trying children in criminal courts.[15]

INFLUENTIAL THEORIES

Policies at the turn of the century were influenced by a number of theories asserting that delinquency is at least partially genetically determined. Henry Goddard and associates asserted that delinquents were feebleminded. Goddard classified those with a mental age of two years or lower as idiots, those with a mental age of three to seven as imbeciles, and morons with mental ages from eight to 12. Other psychologists replicated Goddard's studies and supported the notion that delinquency was the result of feeblemindedness, which was hereditary. William Healey and Augusta Bronner maintained that the vast majority of delinquents' parents were alcoholics and criminals.[16] Goddard and others supported sterilization of the lower end feebleminded, as they believed these people did not know right from wrong. The eugenics policies that developed from this line of thinking were practiced throughout the 1920s and upheld by the Supreme Court until the 1960s. In 1927, the Supreme Court upheld a Virginia law mandating sterilization of inmates in state mental institutions. The American Eugenics Society formed in 1923, eventually having 29 chapters across the nation. Over 64,000 people were subject to forced sterilization before the law was prohibited.

Although the early courts did not keep clear records regarding who was designated feebleminded, records from reformatories and other help agencies indicate the majority were poor white girls and immigrants.[17] Clearly, there was tremendous elitism and racism woven into the practice of designating someone feebleminded. However, some black leaders supported the practice of forced sterilization. W.E.B. Du Bois and Marcus Garvey argued that sterilization would help reduce the suffering of black people. Some proponents maintained that forced sterilization was actually in the female's best interest. "Concerned with race suicide and the mongrelization of races, some psychologists and public reformers, too, pointed out that sterilization protected society, as well as the feebleminded themselves, who were vulnerable to unscrupulous males."[18]

PROVISIONS OF THE JUVENILE COURTS

The 1899 Illinois Juvenile Court Act that established the first separate court for juveniles defined a delinquent child as any minor under the age of 16 who violated a state law or city or village ordinance. Capital felonies remained under the jurisdiction of the adult courts. Six separate categories defined the dependent and neglected child: a child who is destitute, homeless, or abandoned; a child who lacks proper parental care or guardianship; a child who habitually begs or receives alms; a child found living in a house of ill fame or with a vicious or disreputable person; a child whose home is unfit for a child; and a child under the age of eight found peddling or selling any article, singing or playing instruments in the street, or providing public entertainment.[19] The Illinois statue also prohibited children under the age of twelve from being committed to a jail or held at a police station. Separate provisions for delinquent, dependent, and neglected youth were included, and judges were provided a great deal of discretion in the disposition of youth. Most commonly, judges assigned a juvenile to probation, followed by commitment to an orphanage, foster home, or some other form of guardianship. An alternative was to commit a juvenile to a training school (for males) or an industrial school (for females) until age 21. Although legislation typically attempted to differentiate between delinquent, dependent, and neglected youth, these terms were not well defined in many states. Consequently, the legal distinction between the terms became blurred, leading to a number of civil liberty issues in later decades.[20]

Following the notion that juveniles were developmentally different from adults, the new juvenile courts used different terminology, different procedures, and different facilities. Colorado Judge Ben Lindsey wanted to replace the word *court* completely, referring to them as "institutions for human relations."[21] Juvenile court rooms were separate from adult court rooms. Even furniture was scaled down to "child's size," although many of the teenagers who came before the court could barely squeeze into them.[22] The word "adjudication" replaced "trial," and pre-trial and sentencing were referred to as pre-adjudication and disposition, respectively. Juveniles were also charged differently than adults. Rather than being charged, a juvenile was brought before the court based on a petition that could be initiated by a variety of state agents and private parties. A juvenile was not "arrested" based on the petition; rather, he or she was "taken into custody."[23] Court reformers also borrowed medical lingo to describe their pet project. Judges were doctors, courtrooms were the doctors clinics, offenders were patients, and they were to be treated for getting sick.[24] An elaborate screening, or intake, process, replaced the traditional legal steps of appearing before a magistrate, the preliminary hearing, arraignment, and plea negotiations.

Once in the court system, children had no due process rights, as juvenile processes were considered civil, not criminal. No lawyers were needed, it was thought, as the judge and probation officer were charged with being surrogate parents and counselors. In fact, legal counsel was discouraged, as juvenile court advocates maintained lawyers would muddy up the process. Juveniles were "adjudged," not found guilty. It was hoped that this change in terminology would reduce the stigma associated with being convicted of a crime.[25] Although most of the offenders that appeared before the early courts were 12 to 18 years old, court supporters often called them, "boys and girls," "lads," and "needy little ones."[26] In another attempt to avoid stigma, juvenile court proceedings were closed to the public, unlike open court hearings.[27]

Even the physical layout of the courts was supposed to differ from the criminal courts, although this is typically not true today. The intent was to foster a closer relationship between child, the parents, and the judge, as well as to be less intimidating, the child savers designed a courtroom that often had no elevated judge's bench. Oftentimes, judges wore professional office attire rather than the more formal robes. The tone of the court was to be more like a guidance clinic than a courtroom.[28]

The founders of the courts did not see juveniles as criminally responsible, as they lacked the capacity for reasoning, moral understanding, and judgment required for blameworthiness. According to Denver Juvenile Court judge Ben Lindsey, "laws against crimes are as inapplicable to children as they would be to idiots."[29] Early sociologists, Edith Abbott and Sophonisba Breckenridge, both involved in establishing the courts, saw the state as a "sorrowing parent … no longer a power demanding vindication or reparation."[30]

An important innovation in the new courts was the integration of preventive and diagnostic goals. Prior to the establishment of juvenile courts, the primary goal of trying children and youth, as with adults, was discerning the truth of the charges. The juvenile court altered both the nature and purpose of children's courtroom appearances. Literally, accused children were kept out of the courts whenever possible. Ideally, a probation officer would investigate the home situation of a child or adolescent of whom a complaint was filed. If this informal handling of the situation was not effective, the child and his or her family were brought together to the court. Once in court, children and adolescents were to be treated far differently than adults. Rather than discerning the factual truth, the goal was to understand why the juvenile offended. The judge, relying largely on reports from the probation officer, was charged with eliciting all pertinent information from anyone close to the child, including parents, teachers, social workers, and the like.[31]

Another major addition to the juvenile court was the installation of psychiatric clinics.[32] As noted, many of the emerging theories in criminology were focused on psychological factors, especially one's intellect. A group called the Juvenile Protective League very much supported the idea of individualized treatment. The group selected Dr. William Healey, a Freudian theorist, to study some 500 juvenile court clients over 4 to 5 years to determine the causal factors for delinquency.[33] In 1909, the Juvenile Protective League established the Juvenile Psychopathic Institute (JPI), with Healy as its director. The Institute claimed their mission, in part, was to discern the influence of mental or physical defects or abnormality on delinquency.[34] Healey suggested that,

while there were thousands of causes of delinquency, parenting and hereditary factors were the most important. At JPI, Healey and colleagues used
a battery of tests to assess young people, many of which they had devised
themselves.[35]

Another unique feature of the juvenile court movement was the establishment of separate detention facilities for various types of offenses. Prior to the
turn of the century, accused children awaited trial in jails with adults. Now,
reformers contended separate facilities were required for diagnostic, educational, and punitive reasons. While awaiting trial, doctors and other personnel
could examine offenders and provide them academic and moral instruction.[36]
Initially, however, the Chicago legislation allotted no public monies for establishing a detention home. One was eventually located more than two miles
from the County Building, where sessions were held. Transportation was a
significant concern. Cook County donated an old omnibus and two horses to
transport children twice weekly to court sessions, but the bus soon began to
fall apart. After six weeks of hassles, a resolution was found when the Juvenile
Court Committee (JCC) bought their own bus. The bus was too heavy for the
horse, so the JCC got a retired fire department horse. This horse was too fast,
so the JCC eventually bought another horse.[37]

Some maintain that the court's big success was in separating juveniles from
adults. In the two years prior to the enactment of the juvenile court bill,
more than 1,700 children were sent to adult jails. In the two years after the
court opened, only 60 children were sent to adult jails.[38] Transfer of juveniles
involved in the most serious crimes to adult courts occurred approximately 1
percent of the time at the inception of the courts.[39] Between 1897 and 1899,
1,705 children had been incarcerated in the Cook County, Illinois, jail with
adults. Immediately after the inception of the Juvenile Court, those numbers
decreased. Between 1900 and 1902, only 60 children were jailed.[40]

Another innovation, although not frequently enforced, authorized holding
liable neglectful and malicious adults for juvenile delinquency. Building on
the idea that parenting was the ultimate source of criminality, the idea was to
deter "bad" parenting. One way this was done was through the requirement
that offenders and their parents or guardians be tried together. Parents held
liable for their child's delinquency might be fined, required to pay for their
child's time in the reformatory, or even imprisoned.[41] Interestingly, the idea
of holding parents accountable for the actions of their children recirculated
in the 1990s.

Yet another major innovation of the juvenile courts was the widespread use
of probation. Rehabilitation in one's own home, rather than in a reformatory,
was preferable. Detention was still an option, but reformers saw little need
for first-time offenders to be incarcerated. An institution, they argued, was an

artificial childrearing arrangement and could not, by nature, rear children as well as a family could.[42] Probation also centered on the belief that offenders, especially children, should be given a second chance.[43] Many considered the probation officer the most important role in the courts, as it was the probation officer who had the most personal contact with the child. Officers were given great latitude to involve themselves in every aspect of the child's life in order to discover the temptations, the bad examples, and the opportunities for the individual. A jack of all trades, the officer was also expected to instruct children and their families on child care and household management, preach moral and religious values, and reprimand them when these lessons were not demonstrated.[44] The Children's Bureau also recommended that probation officers consult physicians if they saw some type of illness in their charges, and take youth on trips to the zoo, to parks, and to the country. They explained being a probation officer was not just a job, it was a "spiritual thing."[45] Some scholars have described early probation officers as the origin of the "therapeutic state" Sadly, caseloads in the early years, as they are today, were far too high for probation to be as successful as possible. Since the legislatures generally did not provide adequate, if any, funding for the new courts, caseloads for the few probation officers in each county were tremendously high. In Chicago, probation officers were assigned between 50 and 150 children.[46]

Probation was very racially segregated. From the outset, black and white probation officers were hired, but they were not allowed to work in racially different communities.[47] Officers of one race were generally not allowed to visit homes of children of another race.[48] There was concern over the training of probation officers as well. In 1905, new legislation called for the creation and implementation of a merit examination for probation officers. All current officers were also required to take the test.[49] Chicago implemented their first test for those seeking to be probation officers in 1912. The test included such questions as, "What is a juvenile delinquent?" and, "Why do you want this job?" Only 81 of 900 passed. One applicant defined a juvenile delinquent as a "no-account bum," but was hired regardless.[50]

In selecting probation officers, reformers emphasized social work training, and by 1920, probation was generally seen as a form of social work. It was also at this time that social work became distanced from sociology. Social workers emphasized the emotional and mental sources of delinquency, and reformers warned against making social work "too theoretical" by too close connections to universities. Sociology's tendency to emphasize groups was seen as antithetical to the individualized case study method preferred by social workers. Social work's links with psychology grew after World War I, when shell-shocked soldiers were successfully treated by psychiatrists and psychologists.[51]

Since there really was no articulated job description, probation officers regularly met with the Juvenile Court Committee and then developed their own understanding of their charge.[52] When innovative and caring people are allowed to do their own thing, with guidance and supervision, it might work. But when officers are largely uneducated, overworked, and undercompensated, the lack of clear job description could be a major concern. In 1923, Mary Edna McChristie, a probation officer, estimated that less than 7 percent of the over 300 juvenile courts at the time actually followed the rehabilitative philosophy intended for probation.[53]

Probation was not necessarily a new concept. The first probation system was set up in Massachusetts in the 1840s. Boston shoemaker John Augustus convinced local magistrates to allow him to supervise or to help place first-time offenders in foster homes. Augustus first received a drunk who would otherwise have been sent to the drunk tank.[54] Probation for juvenile delinquents also started in Massachusetts prior to the Civil War, when police courts released delinquent boys to Rufus Cook, an agent of the Children's Aid Society.[55] In 1869, the state created the position of Visiting Agent in the Board of State Charities to investigate the social and family background of juveniles accused of crimes and to supervise and place them after trial. Although there may not have been evidence that probation was actually any more effective than other means, it was indeed less costly.[56] By 1891, the Massachusetts juvenile probation system was so entrenched that it required criminal courts to appoint probation officers in juvenile cases.[57] Overuse of reformatories, it was said, allowed parents to shirk their responsibilities for childrearing, allowed less dangerous or even innocent offenders to mix with violent ones, created stigma for those released, was incapable of individualizing treatment, and failed to prepare inmates for life outside the facility.[58]

The benefit of clergy, used in the Middle Ages, was likely the precursor to the concept of probation. Here an offender could avoid the sanction of criminal law by being turned over to the church for punishment. Another precursor was the use in fourteenth century England of "binding over for good behavior," or recognizance.[59]

Highlighting their faith in science, reformers hoped the court would demonstrate why juveniles committed offenses, then would alleviate those reasons. According to one chief probation officer, writing in 1907, "Every Juvenile Court is a laboratory. Every one of its sessions is a clinic—of priceless value to science and society."[60]

Contrary to popular conception, the juvenile courts did not do a number of things. Rather than a detailed description, the juvenile court act of 1899 served more as a blueprint. Consequently, the court opened without several of the provisions reformers wanted. The initial court had open hearings, a public record, no complaint system or other means to control the court calendar, and no public funds to pay the salaries of probation officers or to maintain a detention facility.[61] Perhaps least bothersome at the time were the open hearings and public record, as reformers used these opportunities as free publicity to share with the public the mission of the court.[62]

Importantly, the concept of a status offense emerged from these pieces of juvenile legislation. A juvenile involved in a status offense has not violated a penal law but has some "condition," has been in the "vicinity of," or in a "relationship with" parents, peers, or others that might *lead to* delinquency. There is no adult counterpart to the status offense, although laws against vagrancy and loitering are similar. By establishing status offenses, the notion was they could "nip in the bud" any delinquency.[63] Status offenses can include proscriptive and prescriptive rules. Proscriptive rules are those that prohibit certain behaviors, such as drinking alcohol under a specified age. Prescriptive rules dictate what children are required to do, such as mind the commands of their parents or guardians.[64] The concept of the status offense can be traced through antiquity. The *Analects* of Confucius require a child to obey his parents and elders. Roman law afforded fathers sole authority over the life and death of children, and the Old Testament is filled with passages requiring filial obedience. In 1606, the Massachusetts Bay Colony adopted language from Deuteronomy authorizing the death penalty for "stubborn and rebellious" children under the age of 16.[65] In reality, most early juvenile courts abdicated responsibility for abused children to privately run charities or child welfare services.[66]

It was not only the courts that dealt with delinquent youth, though. In fact, police, as they still do, had much more contact with young people. In the time period between 1890 and 1940, the primary function of police within the juvenile system was to determine which youth were to be petitioned to the court. Outspoken judges criticized the way the police dealt with youth. For instance, Denver Juvenile Court Judge Ben Lindsey said the police use, "fear, degradation, and punishment."[67] The courts often relied heavily on the police. Between 1919 and 1930, serious offenses constituted only 11 percent of complaints investigated by Chicago Police Probation Officers (PPOs), whereas the misdemeanor larceny made up 21 percent. PPOs were most likely to deal with cases on their own than to send them to juvenile court. Between 1918 and 1930, PPOs decided 89 percent of the cases brought to their attention themselves. Child welfare reformers soundly criticized them for this. By the 1940s, arrest became far more popular, and was more often than not reserved for youth of color. In 1940, Hispanic male youth were only 8 percent of the population of Los Angeles, but constituted 32 percent of all boys arrested by the Los Angeles Police Department. "Rather than make the (sometimes impossible) effort to sort out which Hispanic youths were responsible for which alleged offenses, the LAPD erred on the side of arresting them early and often and letting the juvenile court decide how best to deal with particular individuals." Police made detention decisions far more frequently than did the courts.[68]

CONCERNS ABOUT THE COURTS

Although juvenile court acts were "on the books," reality was that many were a far cry from exacting the ideals set out by the court creators. In fact, many seemed to be juvenile courts in name only. Children were sometimes confined in adult jails, less than half of courts reporting in 1920 had a probation service, and psychiatric services were available in only 7 percent of the courts.[69] A U.S. Children's Bureau study in 1920 found that only 16 percent of the juvenile courts had separate calendars for juvenile proceedings or had an official probation service. In 1926, more than 80 percent of the juvenile courts failed to meet the minimum standards set forth by the Children's Bureau.[70]

The early courts did not completely exclude trying juveniles as adults. Many states permitted juvenile court judges to transfer cases.[71] Even in the "heyday" of juvenile justice progressivism, the philosophy that the court was there to assist the child was more rhetoric than reality. For instance, in the first year after the Illinois Juvenile Court began, Judge Richard S. Tuthill sent 37 juveniles to adult courts.[72]

Clearly, delineating the difference between adult and juvenile courts was especially difficult in some areas. Rural counties often lacked social services, including probation officers. In the early years, few counties had full-time staff. In 1940, just over one-third of Illinois counties employed a probation officer.[73]

One problem in the early stages of the Chicago court was the failure to provide for any means of limiting the court's caseload. Under the Juvenile Court Act, a judge was required to hear all cases in which a petition had been filed. Because "any reputable person" in the county could file a petition, it was difficult to limit the number of cases the judges were sworn to hear. Most were not necessarily worthy of the court's attention. The complaint system emerged as a method of docket control. Under this system, individuals made a complaint to the probation office, which would then investigate and determine if the complaint merited judicial attention. This seemed to be effective; in 1912 it was estimated that only one quarter of complaints led to actual petitions.[74]

Although almost every state had passed legislation authorizing a juvenile system of some sort, in some areas actual reform was slow to come. Juvenile justice reforms were far slower to come in the South. Black children were still being held in adult jails well into the twentieth century, and many were placed on chain gangs or released into the convict lease system. Racism is at least part of the reason for the disparate treatment, and was clear in the bigger cities of the North as well.

Advocates generally dismissed early concerns about civil liberties and the treatment of juveniles, as they claimed any effect of juvenile court treatment was inevitably less harmful than involvement in the criminal courts.[75] Although support for the courts was generally widespread, some did express concern about their constitutionality. The preeminent decision in this regard was *Commonwealth v. Fisher* in 1905. Frank Fisher had been committed to the Philadelphia house of refuge, and his attorney's maintained his incarceration was unlawful on three grounds. First, that he had not received due process in the way he was brought to court. Second, Fisher was not provided a jury trial. Third, Fisher's indeterminate sentence to the reformatory was a form of age-based discrimination. The appellate court of Pennsylvania rejected these arguments. The court held that due process was not relevant as long as the government's intentions were benevolent. A jury trial was not required, the appellate court determined, because the goal of the court was to prevent trial. The appellate court rejected the discrimination claim, contending that *parens patriae* allows the court to exercise it's power over children, just as a parent exercises restraint of their children.[76]

Then, as today, juvenile court judges can either be lauded or derided. Certainly intentions were good for most. In 1922, C.C. Carstens, Director of the Child Welfare League of America, outlined four essential elements of a juvenile court judge. First, a judge was to be patient, even with the "stupidest parent" and the "meanest youngster." Second, the majority of children should be sent home, and a skilled probation officer was to assist him or her and his or her family in fitting in to society. Third, no publicity was to be involved in the courts, as privacy was paramount. Fourth, the court was to be allied with other social service agencies in the community.[77] Clearly, not all juvenile court systems had these features, nor did all judges embrace these goals.

Gender Inequality

Until the end of the nineteenth century, the image of the female delinquent was that of the "fallen woman," in opposition to the male delinquent, who was generally seen as a nurtured criminal. Female delinquency, then, was perceived as "innate moral perversity."[78] Female Progressive era reformers sought to protect girls from sexual predators, generally older men who would make them white slaves, but at the same time, the reformers ignored sexual exploitation of young black girls as well as incest in patriarchal family structures. When young females were victims of sexual abuse, it was, like today, more commonly at the hands of male relatives. Simultaneously, families used the courts to control their daughters and to reinforce "proper" gender roles. The vast majority of males involved in statutory rape cases, however, were not older men but young ones of similar class as the female.[79]

Gender discrimination was a routine feature of the juvenile courts. In 1910, 81 percent of the girls brought to the court were there because "their virtue was in peril if it has not already been lost."[80] Part of the issue was that it took 14 years to get the first female at the judicial level, and few services were available for females. In 1913, the first woman assistant judge, Mary Bartelme, convened a girl's court to hear cases regarding delinquent and dependent girls. The court was closed and all personnel were female. Bartelme spent considerable time with each girl and her family, trying to understand the family dynamics. She was also very adept at discerning whether the parents were using the courts to assert their authority, or whether the young lady's rebellion might have been a sign of abuse or neglect.[81] Bartelme also established Mary's Clubs, places where girls who were unable to return to their parents' homes could go in lieu of institutions. The first two Mary's Clubs, opened in 1914 and 1916, were open only to white girls. A third Mary's Club in 1921 allowed black girls.[82] The decade between 1910 and 1920 saw the opening of 23 new facilities for female delinquents, in contrast to only five that were opened in each of the prior decades since 1850.[83]

Despite efforts by the Colored Women's Clubs of Chicago to offer social services to black adults and youth, black dependent children were more likely to be placed in facilities or jails. In 1913, the Juvenile Protection Association reported that one-third of the girls in the Cook County jail were African American. In 1923, 16 percent of the girls at the Geneva Reformatory were black, yet they comprised only two percent of the Illinois population at the time.[84]

An investigation of court records from Chicago, San Francisco, New Haven, and Milwaukee revealed that girls were treated more harshly than boys, and were more likely brought to the court for issues involving sexual exploration.[85] Girls were most frequently status offenders, typically brought before the courts as "incorrigible." Sixty to seventy percent of the girls who appeared before the Chicago court between 1904 and 1927 were first-time offenders.[86] The majority of females were charged with the vague, "immorality" or "incorrigibility." To be dubbed immoral did not even mean she had engaged in any type of sex act; rather, it meant she "showed signs," such as her appearance and her conversation, which indicated she either had or might in the future. Given that the vast majority of juveniles appearing before the court (both males and females) were children of immigrants, the potential for bias was tremendous. The label of immorality also included staying away from home, associating with those of "dubious character," going to dance houses, fornicating, returning home late at night, masturbating, using obscene language, riding in automobiles without a chaperone, and acting lascivious.[87]

Regarding sanctions, boys were far more likely to receive probation than girls. Girls were more likely to be committed to a detention facility, typically a lengthier and more coercive form of sentencing. In Chicago between 1899 and 1909, 59 percent of boys appearing before the court received probation compared to 37 percent of girls. Fifty percent of the girls were committed to reformatories, in contrast to 20 percent of the boys.[88] Girls charged with some type of sexual delinquency were far more likely to be institutionalized than were boys with similar charges, since this was considered more dangerous. "Embedded in those deliberations were the images of victims, good girls whose paths had forked, and sexualized demons who were a danger not just to themselves but to society."[89]

Although many see the role of female reformers as a liberating one, these women did not always use their power benevolently. Females were still subject to invasive questions about their sexual activity, invasive medical procedures when incarcerated, and an overall surveillance of their sexuality.[90] For instance, every alleged female delinquent in the Milwaukee Juvenile Courts was subject to a vaginal exam. An intact hymen was not adequate evidence of virginity; doctors sometimes self-diagnosed that a girl had masturbated and thus was sexually deviant and in need of state intervention.[91] "Girls' bodies matters as much in 1900 as in 2000: girls required help to save themselves for marriage and children, which ultimately supported white racial progress and patriarchy along the way. Whenever a girl used vile language, masturbated, or indulged in lascivious thoughts, the court intervened."[92] The courts investigated more serious sexual misconduct in ways that went far beyond obtaining evidence. They suggest that "sheer titillation" must have been the goal. It was customary in cases in which females were found to be sexually active to blame the mother.[93]

Character-building efforts also differed greatly for males and females. While sports and clubs were being developed for females in the Progressive era, the juvenile justice system was the primary effort to "guide," or control, females. Campaigns to protect females' morality weren't novel in the late 1800s and early 1900s; rather, what was new was the broadened scope and their involvement of the state. How were females deemed sexually deviant to be rehabilitated? Isolation was the key.[94] Girls were almost exclusively charged in the new juvenile courts with some form of status offense, typically "sexual precocity," and were often punished more harshly than boys involved in more serious criminal behavior.[95]

When in detention, girls received education on character building and morals, as well as academic subjects. Girls were awakened at 5 A.M. to clean, cook, and clear breakfast, and prepare vegetables for dinner. Girls were taught sewing and needlework, table manners, cooking, and housekeeping. Their literacy education consisted of writing letters of remorse to judges and letters home, which were monitored.[96]

Essentially, there were four primary goals of female reformatories in the Progressive era. Males were to be isolated from the sexually promiscuous females. This was also said to force the females to "regulate" their sexual favors until marriage. Females were to be released into new social settings where they could supposedly get a fresh start in their search for a mate. Rehabilitative efforts followed gender stereotypes. Females were instructed in domesticity, including personal hygiene, cottage upkeep, and cooking.[97] Further, some have argued the female reformatories were a tool of the eugenics movement, in that the institutionalization of a large number of immigrant females was said to help keep America's "genetic fund" pure. Mental testing was conducted in reformatories, starting in the 1910s, in order to discern which inmates were so inferior that they were to be sterilized.[98] In general, Progressive era reformers saw female delinquents as less amenable to change through informal means, like probation. Since sexuality was the primary focus, more harsh treatment of female delinquents was suggested because this was "adult" behavior.[99]

Racial and Class Inequality

Without a doubt, the continued influx of immigrants shaped the Progressive movement in the later stages. At the start of the twentieth century, 60 percent of the residents in the nation's 12 largest cities were foreign born or had parents that were, and in some cities, like Saint Louis, Chicago, Cleveland, Detroit, New York, and Milwaukee, the number exceeded 80 percent.[100] In addition, mass migration of African Americans from the South created concerns about how these transplants would fit in. According to Richard S. Tuthill, the first judge of the Cook County court, the court would prevent youth from being "branded in the opening years of its life with an indelible strain of criminality."[101] Despite these intentions, the child savers feared that young people in the "foreign colonies" were "un-American," and felt their role was to Americanize them.[102] It is clear that non-whites and foreign children constituted the bulk of the caseload in the earliest courts, in particular in the Midwest. More than 90 percent of the children brought to the Milwaukee juvenile court between 1907 and 1911 were born to European immigrants, with 75 percent being German or Polish. Rates of foreign-born youth before the early Chicago courts were slightly less, but still high at 72 percent.[103]

In the quarter-century before World War I, 18 million immigrants entered the United States, mainly from southern and eastern Europe. By 1920 immigrants and their children formed between 50 and 75 percent of the population of many major cities.[104] Mass migration of blacks to the northern states also altered the population of major cities. Between 1910 and 1920, more than 500,000 blacks migrated to northern states, and an additional 750,000 did so in the 1920s.[105]

In Chicago, the number of black youth appearing before the courts increased at a faster rate than did the population between 1903 and 1930. In 1927, more than 20 percent of the court's cases involved black youth.[106] The court reported that it needed to handle these cases differently, as "The difficulty of providing adequate care for the dependent and neglected colored children constitutes one of the greatest problems with which the court has to deal. The situation is complicated by a lack of resources in the community comparable with those available for white children in the same circumstances. Practically no institutions are found in the community to which this group of colored children may be admitted."[107] Black youth adjudicated delinquent had to be sent to the state-run St. Charles School. St. Charles would not allow parole for youth who lacked a suitable home into which they could be returned, meaning that, very quickly, one-quarter of the inmates at St. Charles were black.[108] Options for dealing with Black female youth were even more limited. The State School for Girls at Geneva was the only place black girls were accepted, and girls were often held elsewhere for six months before a space was available.[109]

In addition to being a testing ground for new philosophies, the courts were a literal dumping ground. They were the place where children and parents who could not perform in "acceptable" ways in the broader society ended up.[110] Critics of the courts contended that, rather than reduce the number of young people involved with the law, "It is quite likely that *more* youth were incarcerated *after* each reform than *before* it."[111] "The juvenile court movement went far beyond a concern for special treatment of adolescent offenders. It brought within the ambit of government control a set of youthful activities that had been previously ignored or dealt with on an informal basis."[112] These offenses included drinking, sexual activity, begging, frequenting dance halls and movies, fighting, and being out late night. It is not surprising that these activities were more common among working-class and immigrant families, and, once arrested, these juveniles were then wards of the state.[113]

CONCLUSIONS

Although innovative in many ways, it is clear from this brief history that the new courts began with many problems. These problems became more apparent in the next era, as the competing attitudes about youth vacillated significantly from the 1920s through the 1950s.

NOTES

1. Watkins, J. (1998). *The juvenile justice century.* Durham, NC: Carolina Academic Press.

2. Grossberg, M. (2002). Changing conceptions of child welfare in the United States, 1820–1935. In M. Rosenheim, F. Zimring, D. Tanenhaus, & B. Dohrn (Eds.). *A century of juvenile justice* (pp. 3–41). Chicago, IL: The University of Chicago Press.

3. Tanenhaus, D. (2002). The evolution of juvenile courts in the early twentieth century: beyond the myth of immaculate construction. In M. Rosenheim, F. Zimring, D. Tanenhaus, & B. Dohrn (Eds.). *A century of juvenile justice* (pp. 42–73). Chicago, IL: University of Chicago Press.

4. Grossberg (2002)

5. Getis, V. (2000). *The juvenile court & the progressives.* Urbana, IL: University of Illinois Press.

6. Knupfer, A. (2001). *Reform and resistance: Gender, delinquency, and America's first juvenile court.* New York: Routledge.

7. Wooden, K. (2000). *Weeping in the playtime of others* (2nd ed.). Columbus, OH: Ohio State University Press.

8. Knupfer (2001).

9. Ibid.

10. Getis (2000).

11. Rosenheim, M., Zimring, F., Tanenhaus, D., & Dohrn, B. (Eds.). (2002). Preface. *A century of juvenile justice.* Chicago, IL: The University of Chicago Press.

12. Watkins (1998).

13. Grossberg (2002).

14. Wooden (2000), p. 26.

15. Zimring (2002). The common thread: Diversion in the jurisprudence of juvenile courts. In M. Rosenheim, F. Zimring, D. Tanenhaus, & B. Dohrn (Eds.). *A century of juvenile justice* (pp. 142–157). Chicago, IL: The University of Chicago Press.

16. Knupfer (2001).

17. Ibid.

18. Ibid., p. 38.

19. Watkins (1998).

20. Ibid.

21. Sealander, J. (2003). *The failed century of the child.* Cambridge: Cambridge University Press, p. 22

22. Ibid.

23. Watkins (1998).

24. Sealander (2003).

25. Watkins (1998).

26. Sealander (2003).

27. Watkins (1998).

28. Ibid.

29. Cited in Scott, E. (2002). The legal construction of childhood. In M. Rosenheim, F. Zimring, D. Tanenhaus, & B. Dohrn (Eds.). *A century of juvenile justice* (pp. 113–141). Chicago, IL: The University of Chicago Press, p. 117

30. Breckenridge, S., & Abbott, E. (1912). *The delinquent child and the home.* New York, p. 205.

31. Schlossman, S. (1977). *Love and the American delinquent.* Chicago, IL: University of Chicago Press.

32. Tanenhaus (2002).

33. Krisberg & Austin (1993).

34. Ibid.

35. Knupfer (2001).

36. Schlossman (1977).

37. Tanenhaus (2002).

38. Mintz, S. (2004). *Huck's raft: A history of American childhood.* Cambridge, MA: The Belknap Press of Harvard University Press.

39. Feld, B. (1999). *Bad kids: Race and the transformation of the juvenile court.* New York: Oxford University Press.

40. Ayers, W. (1997). *A kind and just parent: The children of juvenile court.* Boston, MA: Beacon Press.

41. Schlossman (1977).

42. Ibid.

43. Watkins (1998).

44. Schlossman (1977).

45. Sealander (2003), p. 26.

46. Lathrop, J. (1905). The development of the probation system in a large city. *Charities, 13,* 344.

47. Dohrn, B. (2002). The school, the child, and the court. In M. Rosenheim, F. Zimring, D. Tanenhaus, & B. Dohrn (Eds.). *A century of juvenile justice* (pp. 267–309). Chicago, IL: The University of Chicago Press.

48. Grossberg (2002).

49. Ibid.

50. Sealander (2003).

51. Getis (2000).

52. Dohrn (2002).

53. Sealander (2003)

54. Watkins (1998)

55. Schneider, E. (1992). *In the web of class: delinquents and reformers in Boston, 1810s–1930s.* New York: New York University Press.

56. Schlossman (1977).

57. Tanenhaus (2002).

58. Schlossman (1977).

59. Watkins (1998).

60. Getis (2000), p. 49.

61. Tanenhaus (2002).

62. Ibid.

63. Watkins (1998).

64. Teitelbaum, L. (2002). Status offenses and status offenders. In M. Rosenheim, F. Zimring, D. Tanenhaus, & B. Dohrn (Eds.). *A century of juvenile justice* (pp. 158–176). Chicago, IL: The University of Chicago Press.

65. Ibid.

66. Sealander (2003).

67. Wolcott, D. (2001, Winter). "The cop will get you": The police and discretionary juvenile Justice, 1890–1940. *Journal of Social History.* Retrieved March 19, 2006 from: www.looksmarttrends.com/p/articles/mi_m2005/is_2_35/ai?82066734?pi=dyn, p. 5.

68. Ibid.

69. Tanenhaus (2002).

70. Ibid

71. Myers, D. (2005). *Boys among men: Trying and sentencing juveniles as adults.* Westport, CT: Greenwood.

72. Ibid.

73. Dohrn (2002).

74. Tanenhaus (2002).

75. Watkins (1998).

76. Schlossman (1977).

77. Sealander (2003).

78. Schlossman, S., & Wallach, S. (1998). The crime of precocious sexuality: Female Juvenile delinquency in the progressive era. In P. Sharp & B. Hancock (Eds.). *Juvenile delinquency: Historical, theoretical, and societal reactions to youth* (2nd ed., pp. 41–63). Upper Saddle River, NJ: Prentice Hall, p. 43

79. Odem, M. (1995). *Protecting and policing adolescent female sexuality in the U.S., 1885-1920.* Chapel Hill: University of North Carolina Press.

80. Gittens, J. (1994). *Poor relations: The children of the state in Illinois, 1818–1990.* Urbana, IL: University of Chicago Press, p. 117

81. Knupfer (2001).

82. Dohrn (2002).

83. Schlossman & Wallach (1998).

84. Dohrn (2002).

85. Schlossman & Wallach (1998).

86. Knupfer (2001).

87. Schlossman & Wallach (1998).

88. Ibid.

89. Knupfer (2001), p. 94.

90. Odem.

91. Schlossman & Wallach (1998).

92. Lesko, N. (2002, April 30). Making adolescence at the turn of the century: Discourse and the exclusion of girls. *Current Issues in Comparative Education*, 182–191, pp. 183, 185.

93. Schlossman & Wallach (1998).

94. Lesko (2002).

95. Feld (1999).

96. Dohrn (2002).

97. Schlossman & Wallach (1998).

98. Ibid.

99. Ibid.

100. Ibid.

101. Tuthill, R. (1904). History of the children's court in Chicago. In *Children's courts in the United States: Their origin, development, and results.* Washington, DC: Government Printing Office, p. 1.

102. Breckenridge & Abbott (1912), p. 66.

103. Ibid.

104. Mintz (2004).

105. Ibid.

106. Moses, E. (1936). *The Negro development in Chicago.* Washington, DC: Social Science Research Council.

107. Hill, H. (1927). Annual report of the Chief Probation Officer of the Juvenile Court. *Charity Service Reports.* Cook County, Illinois, p. 364

108. Moses (1936).

109. Hill (1927).

110. Schlossman (1977).

111. Lerman, P. (1991). Delinquency and social policy: A historical perspective. In E. Monkkonen (Ed.). *Crime & justice in American history: Delinquency and disorderly behavior* (pp. 23–33). Westport, CT: Meckler Publishing, p. 29

112. Platt (1998), p.12.

113. Ibid.

4

1920s through 1950s

THE 1920s

In the 1920s, delinquency was a major concern. Labor unrest, soldiers returning from World War I, the prohibition movement, and the rise of gangsters were all said to play a role in the increased rates of crime and delinquency. The experiment with prohibition began January 16, 1920. Rather than keep people from drinking, prohibition actually increased problem drinking.[1] Further, prohibition created contempt for the law and fostered corruption. The enforcement of prohibition also facilitated violence and regular weapons usage by young gang members.

Mass production of the automobile was also a factor in delinquency. Because automobiles were now available, drive-by shootings began, transporting of liquor across state lines was made far more convenient, and kidnapping for ransom became common. Although adults were at the heart of the organized crime of the era, many of these gangsters provided opportunities for juveniles. Juveniles participated in crimes such as driving getaway vehicles, being lookouts at the speakeasies, and running messages regarding racketeering, gambling, bribery, or death threats to prostitutes, politicians, or any member of society that was involved.[2]

In 1924, the nation stood in shock as the horrific details of the murder of 14-year-old Bobby Franks were revealed. Eighteen-year-old Richard Loeb and 19-year-old Nathan Leopold lured Franks into a rental car. As they drove away, one of the boys fractured Franks's skull with a chisel. Franks bled to death. Leopold and Loeb then doused Franks' body with acid, so it was less likely to be identified, and dumped it into a culvert. Leopold and Loeb admitted they had no other motive for the crime than to see if they could do it. Leopold told his defense counsel, "The killing was an experiment. It is just as easy to justify such a death as it is to justify an entomologist in killing a beetle on a pin."[3] Both boys were wealthy heirs with extraordinary IQs. "Convinced that they were Nietzschean supermen above ordinary standards of morality, they had thrown bricks through car windshields, started small fires, and engaged in petty thefts before deciding to commit the perfect murder."[4] The Leopold and Loeb case demonstrated that even the most affluent and intelligent could commit heinous crimes, calling into question some of the theories that stressed that delinquency was the result of low IQ.[5]

In the later part of the 1920s, the public began to view the police, courts, and jails as ineffective in preventing or responding to crime and delinquency. This concern continued during the Great Depression. Likewise, the high hopes for the juvenile courts began to fade, as the public learned that many of the supposed features were more lip service than reality. Several studies in the 1920s found that less than 50 percent of the courts had probation services and less than 10 percent conducted mental examinations. By 1940, "treatment" typically meant placing young people in custodial detention. Critics also denounced probation as a panacea, and decried the conditions of detention centers for youth.[6]

In response to these and other criticisms, as well as new, more sociological theories of delinquency, child welfare advocates and court officials began to turn increasingly to preventive approaches. Affording young males organized, supervised, recreational opportunities became a popular means of prevention and early intervention. The Denver Boys Club was started in 1926, and YMCAs and Boy Scouts were popular programs for young men.[7] Under the direction of August Vollmer, Chief of Police in Berkeley, California, new youth bureaus were created to deal especially with policing young people. By 1924, 90 percent of the nation's largest cities had some type of police-sponsored prevention program. The Police Athletic League (PAL) was started in the 1920s.[8]

THE 1930s

During the Great Depression, the public began to read articles that told them young boys were easy lures for gangsters, who "sold" them a life of affluence amidst a sea of woes. Popular films of the era, such as *Little Caesar* (1931), *The Public Enemy* (1931), and *Scarface* (1932) told the public that they could be raising little gangsters. Over 20 million young people attended the movies at least once per week, so there was tremendous concern about their influence.[9]

In 1934, Harvard criminologists Sheldon and Eleanor Glueck published their study *One Thousand Juvenile Delinquents*, which was one of the first systematic studies to evaluate the juvenile courts and found that 88 percent of the boys who had been handled in the Boston Juvenile Court re-offended in the five years following the offense. This study added to the criticisms of the courts. Richard Cabot, professor of Social Ethics at Harvard, went so far as to call the courts, "an appallingly complete and costly failure, a stupendous waste of time, money and effort."[10] A turning point occurred in 1936 when the Gluecks sponsored a symposium detailing various prevention programs for youth. "No longer did leading thinkers and activists consider juvenile courts the primary institutions for fighting delinquency. Rather than bring children into the juvenile justice system, social workers, teachers, law enforcement officials, and others working with children all sought to address the sources of delinquency before kids reached court."[11]

THE 1940s

The 1940s were critical times in the history of juvenile justice. The public continued to lose support for the rehabilitative ideals of the court, in particular as juvenile crime seemed to escalate during World War II. Newspapers and magazines were filled with stories about juvenile crime. In the first three months after the United States entered World War II, juvenile delinquency among all races in New York City increased 10 percent over the corresponding three months of the year previous.[12] During the World War II era, "Parents grew more conscious than ever before that teenagers had, 'been liberated from adult control.' With four out of five high school boys serving in the army after graduation, teen life seemed like a brief interlude before adult responsibilities intruded."[13] Authorities feared that war desensitized children to violence and undermined their respect for authority.[14] "In adjusting to wartime conditions, American youth developed a more autonomous sense of identity. Subject to public demands and criticisms, American adolescents began to assert themselves and create distinctive teenage subcultures with their own garb, hairstyles, dances, language, and values. Teenage boys, particularly in poorer communities, showed their disdain for social conventions by donning zoot suits, modeled on the garb worn by Depression-era gangsters."[15]

Many fathers were away at war, and those that were not, as well as many mothers, were busy at work. Sometimes, like in the Great Depression, children were generally left to fend for themselves.[16] War was said to exacerbate parental neglect.[17] Supposedly boys were acting out because they were denied the guidance of their fathers, who were at war. FBI Director J. Edgar Hoover said that mothers working outside of the home had resulted in lax morals, resulting in more crime and delinquency. Girls were allegedly more delinquent than ever, although their offenses were still generally sexual in nature. Specifically, there was great concern that young ladies would lure, or be lured by, soldiers.[18] In addition to the war, other societal changes were having a major impact on the perception of crime rates. Continued migration to urban areas, coupled with reduced job opportunities for the young and less educated, prompted young men to band together in gangs.[19] Indeed, the number of gangs grew throughout the 1930s and 1940s. One of the earliest Chicano gangs, the White Fence, formed in the 1940s as a means of protection against racist bullying. The White Fence is said to be one of the first to use chains and guns as weapons. In the Northeast, the massive influx of Puerto Ricans into New York City spawned the creation of Puerto Rican gangs, as depicted in the musical and film *West Side Story.* Whereas the gangs of the 1930s were predominantly white, major American cities in the 1940s saw the growth of all-black gangs who were constantly fighting over neighborhood turfs.[20]

In 1943, Mexican gang members, known for wearing so-called zoot suits, clashed with white soldiers for eight nights in what is now called the zoot suit riots. Police arrested more than 600 Mexican American boys and men, most of whom were victims in the debacle.[21] These riots highlighted the growing racial tensions around the country. Another event that demonstrated the nation's racism was the misidentification and trial of several Chicano teenagers for murder in Sleepy Lagoon in 1942. The Los Angeles press did a series of articles on *pachuco* gangs. As public outrage grew, sheriff's officials conducted a sweep through the city's barrios, arresting more than 600 young men in the Sleepy Lagoon case. A grand jury indicted 24 for murder, making the court proceedings one of the largest mass trials in American history. The defendants were referred to in the press as "The Sleepy Lagooners" and then simply as "goons." One sheriff's department expert testified that "total disregard for human life has always been universal throughout the Americas among the Indian population. And this Mexican element feels … a desire … to kill, or at least draw blood." It wasn't until two years later that an appeals court overturned the convictions.[22] A race riot similar to the zoot suit riot occurred just weeks later in Detroit. Like the zoot suit riot, the police arrested a disproportionate number of black males.[23] Military training also taught older adolescent males proficiency and comfort with weapons, which they brought to their cities.[24]

The 1940s were not auspicious years for juvenile justice. Legal advocates began to question whether the informality of the juvenile system was truly helpful to young people. This issue would become very important in the 1960s and is discussed at length in Chapter 5. Courts were understaffed in the 1940s and juvenile justice was simply not a priority.[25] New York City

Mayor LaGuardia made the comment that, "Children needed Borden-Sheffield (milk) rather than Binet-Simon (psychological tests)."[26]

THE 1950s

Nostalgia may paint the 1950s as a more placid time, but it was an era of anxiety. "Let's Face It," read the cover of *Newsweek* in 1956, "Our Teenagers Are Out of Control." Many youths, the magazine reported, "got their fun" by "torturing helpless old men and horsewhipping girls they waylaid in public parks." Newspaper readers learned about 25 Washington, D.C., girls, ages 13 to 17, who formed a shoplifting club; and a seven- and nine-year-old from Arkansas who robbed a filling station. The chief of research at the National Institute of Mental Health warned parents that "no one can tell if a child will turn out to be delinquent five years later." Some children, he explained, "prepare for delinquency pleasantly and quietly."[27] Foreshadowing the moral panics about youth and rap music of the 1980s and video games of the 1990s, many adults in the 1950s feared the impact of comic books on young people.[28] In 1954, Frederic Wertham published a book called *The Seduction of the Innocent,* in which he maintained that comic books caused juvenile delinquency.[29]

One historian explained, "We may recall the 1950s as a time of unlocked doors and stable nuclear families, but the decade of Ozzie and Harriet was also a period of intense anxiety over juvenile delinquency and gangs. Senator Robert C. Hendrickson sounded the alarm in 1954. 'Not even the Communist conspiracy,' he declared, 'could devise a more effective way to demoralize, disrupt, confuse and destroy our future citizens than apathy on the part of adult Americans to the scourge known as juvenile delinquency."[30]

Between 1948 and 1954 the number of youths appearing before juvenile courts increased 58 percent. Like today, it is unclear whether there was actually an increase in delinquent activity, or whether the heightened attention resulted in more arrests.[31]

The panic over juvenile delinquency reflected fears about changes in young people's lives as well as rapid change in the broader society. In speech and appearance, teens seemed increasingly alien as a growing number of middle-class teens adopted values, fashions, and speech associated with the lower and working classes. *Juvenile delinquency* became an umbrella term referring to everything from duck-tail haircuts to murder; but it was gangs that aroused the most heated concern. The term was applied broadly, to street-corner loungers, neighborhood clubs, and packs of roving teens; but in the popular imagination, the word conjured up images of a world of switchblades, zip guns, and schoolyard rumbles, where groups of working-class youth, bearing names like "Vampires," "Dragons," and "Egyptian Kings," defended turf and avenged real and imagined slights.[32]

The number of gangs in big cities exploded after the mid-1940s. Gang conflicts became more about race, and violence increased as ice picks, knives, and homemade guns became the weapons of choice. Movies like *Blackboard Jungle* blamed gangs on the chaos created by war.[33]

NEW THEORIES

The decades addressed in this chapter were pivotal in the development of theories about delinquency. A vast array of views were offered to explain delinquency and to direct policy. As will be evident, these theories furthered the mixed messages of juvenile justice, as they are hardly in agreement about the basic nature of offending.

Individual-Focused Theories

As was noted in the previous chapters, psychological theories had some influence on the early development of the courts. The theories remained very popular in the 1920s and 1930s. Historians have documented the rise in child-guidance clinics through the 1930s that were, in many cases, extensions of the juvenile court.[34]

Perhaps the most significant psychological theory was one not directed overtly at crime and delinquency. Sigmund Freud's psychoanalytic perspective emphasized disruptions in an individual's personal development. According to Freud, much of our development takes place unconsciously. In 1927, Freud hypothesized three personality components. The id represents our instinctual drives, or the "passion principle." The ego is the source of reason and serves to regulate the id's impulses. The superego represents the influence of society. It is our conscience, balancing the id and ego through the imposition of societal norms.[35]

Essentially, Freudian scholars assert that delinquency is the result of underlying conflicts in the personality, many of which are unconscious. Freudian scholars often highlighted the sexual nature of delinquent acts. One of the most important concepts in psychoanalytic theory is the Oedipal Complex. According to Freud, at the ages of two and three, young boys feel a one-sided rivalry with their fathers for their mothers' attention. Resolution of this rivalry results in the development of the superego. Boys who engage in delinquency are the ones who never resolved this issue and hence did not fully develop the superego. Girls, according to Freudian theorists, suffer from penis envy. This envy might result in a masculinity complex in which the female identified with males, which could lead to behavioral problems.[36]

In 1925, August Aichorn applied Freudian theory to explain the case of a 17-year-old who stole alcohol from his father then urinated in the bottles to hide the theft. Aichorn concluded that the urination was a means of getting back at his dad for his affection toward a stepmother. Additionally, Freudian scholars emphasized that delinquency is a disease. Healey and Bronner likened delinquency to tuberculosis. Delinquency is like a symptom of a psychological disorder, like there are symptoms of tuberculosis. W. I. Thomas wrote in *The Unadjusted Girl* (1925), that females manipulated their sexuality to achieve what they wanted. Hence, like the Freudians, Thomas maintained female delinquency was the result of adjustment problems.[37] The field of social work adopted a Freudian perspective in the 1920s, which focused more on the individual offender's feelings and emotions than on attempting to rectify environmental concerns.[38]

In 1941, Hervey M. Cleckley, a neuropsychiatrist, developed the concept of the psychopath. In his book, *The Mask of Sanity,* Cleckley described the psychopath as a moral idiot who cannot feel empathy. Psychopaths are incapable of thinking from another person's point of view. They are often superficially charming, have average or better intelligence, and are chronic liars. They are self-centered, even narcissistic. Psychopaths may be hard to detect initially because of their charm and general agreeableness. Cleckley identified signs of psychopathology early in life. Bed wetting, cruelty to animals, sleepwalking, and fire setting are signs for the very young. In the teenage years, signs include lying, fighting, stealing, and vandalism.[39] In the 1960s, the American Psychiatric Association stopped using the terms psychopath or sociopath, replacing them with antisocial personality.[40]

Like Lombroso earlier, some theorists maintained that specific bodily characteristics could identify delinquents. In the 1940s, William Sheldon argued that he could link a person's body with his or her personality, called somatotyping. Sheldon described three main body types: endomorphs, ectomorphs, and mesomorphs. Endomorphs are soft, fat, gregarious, and jolly. They are the least likely to be involved in delinquency. Ectomorphs are thin and fragile, easily excitable, introverted, and afraid. They are also not very likely to engage in delinquency because they lack self-confidence. Mesomorphs are the most likely to offend. They are athletic, muscular, and adventuresome.[41]

Social Disorganization

In the early part of the twentieth century, Robert Park, Ernest Burgess, and associates from the University of Chicago began mapping crime and delinquency rates in Chicago. These theories came to be known as ecological theories. In the 1920s and 1930s, Clifford Shaw and Henry McKay followed in their footsteps and furthered the development of sociological theories of delinquency. Shaw and McKay measured delinquency rates in Chicago between 1900 and 1906, 1917 and 1923, and 1927 and 1933. They found that delinquency decreased as one moved away from the core of the city. The same results were true when they analyzed the number of males committed to correctional facilities. Follow-up studies in Philadelphia, Boston, Cleveland, and Richmond (Virginia) verified the same pattern for boys and for girls. Shaw and McKay concluded that the core of the city was organized differently than the outer areas, and this differential social organization lead to delinquency.[42]

The idea was that the rapid change in the core areas of a city, such as immigration, migration, and industrialization, prevented the residents from establishing firm social norms and values that constrain delinquency. In addition, communities in flux are less able to develop social control mechanisms that effectively prevent delinquency. It was not just that communities were broken or disorganized, but the University of Chicago sociologists were concerned about broken or disorganized families as well.[43] Interestingly, the theory is typically called social disorganization, although Shaw and McKay did not prefer that terminology. They favored calling these areas differentially socially organized.[44]

Reformers and social workers who spearheaded the settlement house movement in Chicago were some of the earliest and most vocal champions of the ecological view of crime. Hull House founder Jane Addams saw delinquency as the result of a lack of fit between the ways of newly arriving immigrants and the modern means of city life. Consequently, a primary goal of settlement houses was to "Americanize" the foreign-born.[45] Although reformers were aware of these developments, they had difficulty translating them into practice. The courts, they found out, were unable to affect neighborhood instability, family disintegration, and concentrated poverty.[46] Critics, such as Chicago sociologist W. I. Thomas, asserted it was ridiculous to think that any sort of "community center" established by an outside center would make significant community change. Instead, he argued that reformers should organize local self-help groups and encourage local leadership. His ideas took form in the 1932 Chicago Area Project, led by Chicago sociologists Shaw and McKay.[47] The Chicago Area Project is considered to be the genesis of large-scale community efforts to address delinquency. It represented a dramatic shift from the psychological explanations popular at the time.[48] It is discussed in greater detail later in the chapter.

Learning Theories

In 1939, Edwin Sutherland advanced perhaps the most influential criminological theory of all time. Sutherland maintained that crime, like any other behavior, is learned through social interaction. Sutherland argued that offenders learned both the motivation and the methods, the "how-to," from those with whom they had frequent, intense, and lengthy relationships. He called the process differential association. People also are more likely to learn to be delinquent from those whom are most important; that is, the relationships that are priority, such family and close friends.[49] Sutherland's was one of the first theories to address white-collar forms of crime, and was thus very applicable at a time punctuated by organized crime.

The young boy, Stanley, showed how differential association might work in *The Jackroller:* "I was really awed by the bravery and wisdom of the older crooks. Their stories of adventures fascinated my childish imagination, and I felt drawn to them. My timid spirit (you remember I was only eight) wanted to go out and achieve some of the glories for myself.[50] Additionally, he said, "It was a novelty to learn that there were so many crimes and ways of stealing that I had never heard about."[51]

Following the learning theories, it made sense that police, probation, and the juvenile court were allowed great latitude in their attempts to prevent or disrupt negative associations and in helping communities become "more organized."[52] While seemingly benevolent, efforts to intervene with youth often smacked of elitism.

In 1956, Daniel Glaser added an important element to differential association that updated it for the times. Research on the effects of violent television programming began in the 1950s. In 1951, the National Association of Educational Broadcasters surveyed television programming in four large U.S. cities. They found that crime and horror programs constituted 10 percent of program time.[53] Clearly, if individuals learned from the media, they might learn crime and violence from characters on television. Glaser maintained that people might become delinquent because they identify with someone holding delinquent values. Thus his differential identification theory explained how a person might engage in delinquent behavior as a result of their identification with various reference groups. To Glaser, identification was a symbolic process.[54]

Strain Theories

A classic in sociological theory is that of Emile Durkheim. Writing during times of great change in France, Durkheim posited that rapid change can lead to a sense of normlessness, or anomie. When there is change, whether economic crises or prosperity, social regulation is minimized and individuals feel out of place. Durkheim applied this concept to the study of suicide, but not to delinquency. In 1938, Robert Merton applied the concept of anomie to the study of delinquency.[55]

Merton argued that delinquency was the result of a disjuncture between socially promoted goals and the means to achieve them. The most important goal in the United States, according to Merton, is attaining economic success. Although all people are supposed to achieve economic success, legitimate means to achieving them are not equally dispersed. In some areas, people do not accept the so-called legitimate means of achieving economic success. Additionally, there are groups that reject the goal.[56]

According to Merton, there are five adaptations people will make to the disjuncture between goals and means. The most common response, Merton argued, was conformity, whereby people accept both the goals and means. Although they may not actually ever achieve economic success, these people work hard and simply accept their lot. Conformists are not delinquents. Ritualists are slightly different—they may not accept the goal, but they accept the means. In other words, they may recognize that they will never achieve economic success, but they may work hard nonetheless. In fact, ritualists often become consumed with minor details. Rather than being delinquents, ritualists are more likely viewed as odd. Innovators accept the goal of economic success, but do not accept the means. Instead, they attempt to find new ways of achieving the goal. They are most likely to be involved in offenses like theft. Retreatists reject both the goal and the means. They are society's dropouts, and are most prone to drug use. Rebels reject the goals and means, but they seek to replace them with new goals and new means.[57] Rebels are more likely to be involved in property crimes.[58]

In 1957, Gresham Sykes and David Matza expanded strain theory by addressing how an individual might overcome feelings of guilt and responsibility when he or she offends. Their idea, called techniques of neutralization, was that individuals use five types of justification for their action. Although the individual offender might find these techniques legitimate, they are not legitimate in the eyes of the law.[59] Denying responsibility refers to pointing to another source, typically one's background, as the real source of the problem. Claiming that "everyone does it" or "they'll never notice, they're so rich" is called denying injury. Some offenders deny the victim by saying the victim deserved it. Others condemn the condemners. That is, they may argue police were corrupt or were profiling them. Finally, offenders appeal to higher loyalties by arguing that they did it for someone else, as in the case of gang members arguing their gang leaders made them do a drive-by shooting.[60]

Theories Focused on the Lower Class

In the 1950s, a number of theories emerged that stressed that delinquency was largely a lower-class concern. These theories emphasizes that the lower-class males formed subcultures or gangs in which values different from the mainstream culture dominated. In 1955, Albert Cohen asserted that most societal institutions, especially schools, are built with middle-class values. Thus the behavior of young people is measured against a middle-class measuring rod. Middle-class values include: drive and ambition, individual responsibility, self-control, planning, achievement, "wholesome" recreation, and respect for the property of others. When lower-class youth exhibit different values they are judged. As a result, they reject the middle-class values, even becoming hostile toward anyone and anything they see as middle class. Cohen called this process reaction formation. These boys will band together, forming a subculture or gang that reinforces the opposition to the mainstream.[61]

Walter Miller developed a similar theory based on lower-class culture. He maintained, like Cohen, that there are distinct values for males in lower-class cultures. He called these focal concerns. The focal concerns are: trouble, or involvement with run-ins with authorities; toughness; smartness (in regard to outwitting someone on the street); excitement, or thrill-seeking; fate, or the belief that one's future is out of his control; and autonomy, or the idea of being one's "own boss."[62] Miller maintained that these focal concerns lead to delinquency in a number of ways. For one, they take males out of the home, and the absence of a father figure generates delinquent boys. Also, because people have an innate need to belong, if lower-class boys who all hold these values live together and interact, they will reinforce delinquent behavior.[63]

In 1960, Richard Cloward and Lloyd Ohlin blended Merton's strain theory with elements of Sutherland's differential association to create a theory of differential opportunity. They argued that people are fully aware of the class inequalities in the United States. Blocked opportunities generate criminal activity. Yet the type of criminal activity varies by neighborhood because specific characteristics of the community present different opportunities for offending. In essence, they maintained that not only were legitimate opportunities for success blocked, but in many cases illegitimate opportunities were blocked as well. Cloward and Ohlin theorized three types of lower-class gangs. Crime was especially appealing to some young men because no other opportunities were available.[64] Stanley from *The Jackroller* said, "Crimes held lures and adventures for me that nothing else did. There was nothing else open for me."[65]

CONCERNS ABOUT THE SYSTEM

Discrimination against the Poor

It is hardly a surprise that the courts continued to discriminate against the poor during the depression years and beyond. In part, this was due to inadequate training, pay, and prestige for juvenile court judges. Juvenile court judges, from the very beginning of the courts, received less compensation than judges appointed or elected to other courts. They were given no law clerks and were not expected to write opinions. In some states they were not provided law reports or legal periodicals to review.[66] Further, "The workload of a judge, often 100 cases a day in the 1930s, demanded speedy dispositions of the living poor, not unlike disposition of the dead during the plague. Because it was assumed that any judge could do justice to a child, the rotation of judges allowed shuffling of a child's case among as many as a dozen judges over a period of months."[67] One author described the conditions in juvenile courts:

Traditional attitudes toward the poor reached into every crevice in the administration of juvenile justice. Parents seeking aid and youth charged with offenses sat hours in airless waiting rooms. Noisy verbal and physical battles had to be broken up by court attendants. The hard benches on which everyone was forced to sit and the atmosphere, like that in lower Criminal Courts, resembled bullpens more than a court for human beings. When air conditioners were introduced they were first installed in courtrooms and judicial chambers, rather than in the stifling waiting rooms.[68]

Racial Discrimination

Black children in the late 1930s and 1940s were often classified as dull-normal or retarded on the basis of their IQ scores. State schools and many voluntary agencies rejected them for assistance. Finally, in 1967, a federal court held that IQ testing used to place poor black children in school assignments was a violation of the Fourteenth Amendment.[69] Judges in the 1930s were not self-conscious about their biases. Despite a doubling of the black population in New York City between 1920 and 1930, few services or facilities were available for black children. In 1939, only four voluntary agencies in New York accepted black children, and these facilities were segregated and by no means "equal." Only one institution accepted both black and white children.[70] Denials of services were couched in condescending terms. One agency agreed to accept a small black child for foster home care, but only if the mother, who had a darker complexion, agreed not to visit him so he could still "pass."[71]

Abuse in Detention

Stanley from *The Jackroller* discussed the abuse at the detention center: "For making even a little noise or even talking out loud, you would get a beating" (p. 66). "The horrors of that House of 'Corruption' cannot be described. I can only say that when there I lost all respect for myself, felt degenerated and unhuman. I shall never fully recover from the influences of that old south cellhouse."[72]

NEW POLICIES AND PROGRAMS

During the 1920s and 1930s, the approach to policing in many big cities underwent a major shift. The LAPD, for instance, shifted away from their traditional, informal methods to far more aggressive efforts to control youth. They began to utilize the many prevention programs developed in these decades so they could divert those engaged in minor offenses and concentrate their efforts on more serious delinquency.[73] Based on panic over the rapidly growing Latino population, as well as press hysteria about the aforementioned zoot suit riots, the LAPD went after young, Latino males with vigor. Although whites and African American youth were involved in 6 percent combined of the robbery and assault cases sent to court, Latinos were involved in 17 percent of those cases.[74]

Another policing approach with youth was akin to modern-day zero tolerance policing. Likely influenced by social disorganization theory, the Los Angeles Police Department and other police agencies aggressively targeted vagrant youth. In particular, they looked for transient youth who would ride the trains looking for work.[75] Girls were not targeted in the same way because their offenses were not seen as problematic to the degree that boys' were. Most of the offenses committed by girls, like previous decades, were related to their alleged immorality. Girls were most frequently arrested for sexual and social precocity. In contrast to their aggressive tactics with young males, police mostly relied on outside sources to bring female cases to them.[76]

One of the most long-lasting projects, derived from social disorganization theory, is the Chicago Area Project (CAP). It was founded by University of Chicago Sociologist Clifford Shaw in 1931 and began in 1934. The idea was to increase opportunities for youth in the highest crime areas. Community committees were created and charged with improving the physical appearance and recreational opportunities, and developing mentor programs for youth.[77] CAP also utilized young "streetworkers," who attempted to gain acceptance into gangs in order to provide them "curbstone counseling" in how to adhere to mainstream values.[78]

World War II brought about some significant changes to the juvenile justice system. One new program that began during the war involved boys who had already been through the juvenile court system and who had improved their situations while on probation. These young men volunteered for the armed services, and if they were honest about their prior records to recruiting officers, the juvenile courts would usually allow them to join the service. Those offenders whose records prohibited them from joining the service often slipped back into delinquent behaviors.[79]

CONCLUSIONS

As this history documents, concerns about juvenile delinquency and the courts' ability to respond grew throughout the 1920s, 1930s, and 1940s. By the 1950s, the public was convinced juvenile delinquency was out of control, and was skeptical of the courts' capacity to deal with it. As Chapter 5 will show, skepticism grew into outright disbelief in the 1960s.

NOTES

1. Sullum, J. (2003). *Saying yes.* New York: Archer Putnam
2. Mintz, S. (2004). *Huck's raft: A history of American childhood.* Cambridge, MA: The Belknap Press of Harvard University Press.
3. Ibid., p. 213.
4. Ibid., p. 213.
5. Ibid.
6. Wolcott, D. (2005). *Cops and kids: Policing urban America, 1890-1940.* Columbus: Ohio State University Press.
7. Ibid.
8. Bartollas, C., & Miller, S. (1994). *Juvenile justice in America.* New York: Pearson.
9. Wolcott (2005)
10. Ibid., p. 134.
11. Ibid., p. 138.
12. Schramm, G. (1942). The juvenile court in wartime. *Journal of Educational Sociology, 16*(2), 115–123.
13. Mintz (2004), p. 267.
14. Ibid.
15. Ibid., p. 266.
16. Polier, J. (1989). *Juvenile justice in double jeopardy: The distanced community and vengeful retribution.* Hillsdale, NJ: Lawrence Erlbaum Associates.
17. Mintz (2004).
18. Wolcott (2005).

19. Schneider, E. (1992). *In the web of class: delinquents and reformers in Boston, 1810s–1930s.* New York: New York University Press.

20. Schramm (1942).

21. Wolcott (2005).

22. Mintz (2004), p. 272.

23. Wolcott (2005).

24. Schneider (1992).

25. Polier (1989).

26. Ibid., p. 7.

27. Mintz (2004), p. 291.

28. Springhall, J. (1998). *Youth, popular culture and moral panics.* New York: St. Martin's Press.

29. Mintz (2004).

30. Ibid., p. 293.

31. Ibid.

32. Ibid., p. 293.

33. Ibid.

34. Krisberg, B. & Austin, J. (1993). *Reinventing juvenile justice.* Newbury Park, CA: Sage.

35. Shoemaker, D. (1996). *Theories of delinquency.* New York: Oxford.

36. Ibid.

37. Ibid.

38. Bartollas & Miller (1994).

39. Cleckley, H. (1941). *The mask of sanity.* St. Louis: C.V. Mosby.

40. Schmalleger, F. (2005). *Criminology today* (3rd ed.). Upper Saddle River, NJ: Prentice Hall.

41. Holmes, S. & Holmes, R. (2002). *Sex crimes* (2nd ed.). Thousand Oaks, CA: Sage.

42. Shoemaker (1996).

43. Knopfer, A. (2001). *Reform and resistance: Gender, delinquency, and America's first juvenile court.* New York: Routledge.

44. Shoemaker (1996).

45. Testa, F., & Furstenberg, F. (2002). The social ecology of child endangerment. In M. Rosenheim, F. Zimring, D. Tanenhaus, & B. Dohrn (Eds.) *A century of juvenile justice* (pp. 237–265). Chicago, IL: The University of Chicago Press.

46. Ibid.

47. Ibid.

48. Krisberg & Austin (1993).

49. Schmalleger (2005).

50. Shaw, C. (1966). *The jack-roller.* Chicago, IL: University of Chicago Press, p. 57

51. Ibid., p. 58.

52. Watkins (1998). *The juvenile justice century.* Durham, NC: Carolina Academic Press.

53. Slaby, R. (2002). Media violence: Effects and potential remedies. In G. Katzmann (Ed.). *Securing our children's future: New approaches to juvenile justice and youth violence* (pp. 305–337). Washington, DC: Brookings Institute Press.

54. Glaser, D. (1960). Differential association and criminological prediction. *Social Problems, 8,* 6–14.

55. Merton, R. (1938, October). Social structure and anomie. *American Sociological Review, 3,* 672–682.

56. Ibid.

57. Ibid.

58. Shoemaker (1996).

59. Sykes, G. & Matza, D. (1957, December). Techniques of Neutralization: A theory of delinquency. *American Sociological Review, 22,* 664–670.

60. Schmalleger (2005).

61. Cohen, A. (1955). *Delinquent boys: The culture of the gang.* New York: The Free Press.

62. Miller (1958).

63. Shoemaker (1996).

64. Cloward, R., & Ohlin, L. (1960). *Delinquency and opportunity: A theory of delinquent gangs.* Glencoe, IL: Free Press.

65. Shaw (1966), p. 108.

66. Polier (1989).

67. Ibid., p. 4.

68. Ibid., p. 4.

69. Ibid.

70. Ibid.

71. Ibid., p. 138.

72. Shaw (1966), p. 154.

73. Wolcott (2005).

74. Ibid.

75. Ibid.

76. Ibid.

77. Shoemaker (1996).

78. Wolcott (2005).

79. Schramm (1942).

5

1960s through 1980s

INTRODUCTION

"It is sometimes claimed that the history of juvenile justice has been a steady march toward more humane and enlightened conceptions of childhood and democracy, but a more reliable reading of history shows that a period of reform has inevitably led to a period of retrenchment. Or, to express this another way, the history of juvenile justice appears to go through cycles of reform and retrenchment."[1] The cycle begins when the public becomes convinced juvenile crime is a pressing social issue and demands something be done. During the later 1960s through the 1980s, harsh punishments tended to dominate and few lenient options were available. Because there were few lenient·punishment options, many offenders avoid sanction because some believe that harsh sanctions will be even more detrimental. A period of reform then offers more lenient options for youth.[2]

THE 1960s

Similar to the cycle described above, other authors have described three trends or eras in juvenile justice: the beginning rehabilitative era; the libertarian era, and the conservative era. The rehabilitative era began prior to the courts and emphasized the differences between juveniles and adults. The libertarian era, they argued, began in the 1960s with concerns about labeling and unfair treatment. Reformers in this era, while emphasizing that juveniles differed from adults, advocated that young people should receive the same procedural and civil liberties guarantees afforded to adults through the criminal justice system.[3] Other criminologists such as Edwin Schur and David Matza advocated a less-restrictive approach with juveniles. Coming from both the conflict (Chapter 5) and labeling (this chapter) perspectives, Schur and Matza maintained that only chance dictated which offenders would be caught, and that those offenders were often negatively labeled. Those negative labels become a self-fulfilling prophecy. Thus, they asserted that, whenever possible, juvenile offenders should be left alone. When the system did intervene, it should do no more than is necessary.[4]

The Libertarian era started in the 1960s and was marked most notably by a revolution of sorts in the juvenile court system. Building on the criticisms of the previous decades, as well as the dramatic movements for civil rights, a new breed of reformers maintained that the juvenile system was not the ideal parent described on paper. Rather, it was a mess in which young people were neither provided the individualized, rehabilitative focus they were due, nor did they receive the constitutional protections afforded adults in the criminal justice system. Juveniles truly had the worst of both worlds.

The juvenile justice system experienced a turning point in 1967. First came the President's Commission Report, which recommended four reforms: diversion from the formal system, decriminalization of status offense, deinstitutionalization, and due process rights. The President's Commission on Law Enforcement and Administration of Justice reported data suggesting racial disproportionality in the juvenile courts. They also reported few juveniles received legal counsel.[5] Later in that year, *In re Gault* extended due process rights in the juvenile justice system. The Gault decision and the Commission recommendations were largely implemented via the 1974 Juvenile Justice and Delinquency Prevention Act, which tied state compliance to deinstitutionalize status offenders and to remove juveniles from adult prisons to receipt of federal funds.[6]

In addition, new theories helped bring to light the inadequacies of a state-based response to delinquency and helped outline the possibility of a dramatically different form of delinquency prevention and control. Some argued that interventions designed to help often make things worse for juveniles. The Cambridge Sommerville Youth Project, which began in 1939, was designed to help at-risk boys and their families. The project provided counseling, tutoring, and other social services. A 30-year follow-up study found boys in the experimental group were actually more likely than the control group to have been involved in crime. The author of the study maintained this could be due to increased dependency, or the fact that expectations were raised and boys could not reach them.[7]

THE 1970s

The Conservative era began in the mid-1970s. It was a backlash against the perception that things had come too far in favor of offenders and that the consequence was out-of-control delinquents. Christian Parenti has explained how the Nixon/Goldwater campaign introduced a lexicon of fear into politics.

At the heart of this new type of politics was a very old political trope: white racism and the self-fueling fear bred by it. Crime meant urban, urban meant Black, and the war on crime meant a bulwark built against the increasingly political and vocal racial "'other'" by the predominantly white state. The fear of crime became all-American.[8]

The mid-1970s saw the end of the "golden age" of delinquency theory. This was due, in part, to the reduced funding of the Nixon, Ford, and Reagan administrations to theory-based programs.[9] The Conservative era lasted into the 1990s, and by some accounts, has continued to the present.

THE 1980s

In the 1980s, concern that legislation and the courts had swung too far in favor of defendants rights, coupled with a dramatic surge in crime rates, prompted a variety of "get tough" laws and policies. Three trends in the mid-1980s facilitated the vacillation away from the rehabilitative approach and back to the get-tough approach. The growing number of gangs, the emergence of the crack epidemic, and the proliferation of guns, coupled with widespread media attention to juvenile crime, prompted fear and the need to do something serious.[10] The loss of decent-paying jobs for semiskilled workers in various manufacturing injuries after the early 1970s surely contributed to crime rates. The transition to a service economy reduced employment opportunities, in particular for blacks in ghetto areas.[11] The Reagan administration worked to end federal funding of juvenile programs by requesting zero funds for the Office of Juvenile Justice and Delinquency Prevention (OJJDP). asserting that the states were using OJJDP money for other purposes than those required, and that state programs were based on local philosophies and thus did not need federal support.[12]

Additionally, media attention painted the face of violent crime as a young, black one.[13] Arrest rates verify that youth crime was black crime. Since the 1960s, arrest rates for Black youth have been five times greater than for white youth.[14] Between 1986 and 1993, homicide arrests for young whites increased 40 percent, while arrests for blacks accused of homicide increased 278 percent.[15] Yet how much of the increase can be explained by profiling of sorts? Perhaps police began focusing their efforts more on black youth.

High-profile incidents of juvenile offending exacerbated the image that juvenile crime was a minority problem. In 1989, a young woman was severely beaten and sexually assaulted while jogging alone in Central Park in New York. The woman came to be known as the Central Park Jogger, and the attack was so brutal she lost three-quarters of her blood. A group of young men, all of whom were black or Hispanic, were arrested for the assault. Approximately 40 youth were allegedly involved, although only five were prosecuted. All five were found guilty of at least some of the charges against them. In addition to issues of racial profiling, the case highlighted many of the ongoing concerns about juvenile justice. Most notably, there was tremendous concern that the young men were interrogated in inappropriate ways and that media attention pressured the system to act in haste. In 2002, a known sex offender Matias Reyes confessed that he was the one who attacked the jogger. His DNA matched DNA found at the scene.[16]

GETTING TOUGH

In 1978, New York led the "get tough" charge against juveniles when it enacted the Juvenile Offender law that provided for automatic transfer to criminal court, lengthier sentences, and lowered age jurisdiction.[17] The punitive trend continued at the federal level with the 1986 Crime Bill. Just as the 1986 summer legislative season began, newly drafted black basketball star Len Bias died from cocaine overdose before he could play a day for the Boston Celtics. In the July following Bias's death, all three of the major television networks broadcast more than 74 evening news segments about drugs, with more than half of them about crack. Major newspapers and magazines chimed in, calling crack the story of the year.[18] Bias's death and the ensuing moral panic prompted major anti-drug initiatives. The 1986 Anti-Drug Abuse Act authorized mandatory minimum sentences for 29 new offenses. This was the start of the infamous crack versus cocaine disparity—the legislation authorized the same penalty for someone arrested with 500 grams of cocaine as someone with 5 grams of crack. The legislation dramatically increased arrests for users, most of which disproportionately impacted men of color. Police in large cities across the nation conducted sweeps of ghetto areas in which they rounded up black and Hispanic men, most of whom were low-level users.[19]

Starting in the 1980s and persisting to the present, laws and punishments targeting sex offenders have been popular. Many cities have expanded laws limiting where sex offenders can live. For instance, in Pembroke Pines, Florida, sex offenders are prohibited from living within 2,500 feet of schools, parks, school bus stops, and daycare centers. The city is looking into broadening their legislation to cover sex offenders convicted in other states, as it currently only covers Florida offenders. Opponents of this type of law maintain it will be even harder to track sex offenders if there is virtually nowhere left for them to legally reside.[20] Further, there is great concern over what offenses should require registration and the potential stigmatizing impact of registering on youth. These concerns are discussed in greater detail in Chapter 6.

NEW THEORIES

One of the most popular theories of delinquency is Travis Hirschi's Social Bond or Social Control theory. Hirschi began to ask a slightly different question about delinquency. Rather than pondering what made juveniles offend, Hirschi turned the question around and asked, Why don't more juveniles offend? His premise is that all people have the capacity to commit an act of crime or violence, yet many never do. Consequently, research should examine the factors that constrain people from offending, rather than the factors that allow them to. Hirschi posited that social bonds prevent people from acting delinquently and developed four elements of the social bond. Attachment is the psychological and emotional connection people have to others. Commitment is the investments we have in conformity. That is, it represents the losses we will incur were we to offend, such as time, money, and status. Involvement is our participation in legitimate activities. Much like the old adage, "Idle hands are the devil's workshop," the idea is that those who are involved in legitimate, conventional activities will not have time (nor the interest) to get involved in illegitimate ones. Belief refers to the degree to which people believe in the conventional value system.[21]

The 1960s saw renewed interest in Labeling Theories. Howard Becker proposed that deviance was largely the result of the actions of rule enforcers, or those people who targeted the powerless for application of laws.[22] Labeling theory argues that individuals acquire certain labels or stigmas through social interaction and that negative labels in turn often lead to deviance and crime. The idea is that labels become a self-fulfilling prophecy, whereby juveniles see little to lose in offending because they believe others already see them that way.

Conflict theory became a popular sociological theory during the 1960s. Distrust of government and concern about the inadequacy of "official" crime statistics helped garner support for a dramatically different view. Conflict theorists contended that the elite used the criminal justice system to control the lower class and maintain the status quo. Conflict theory began to have a strong impact on criminology in the 1970s. Specifically, it helped explain white-collar crime in an era in which Watergate and other high-profile scandals had shown other theories to be inadequate.[23]

Conflict theory originated in the work of Karl Marx and his successors, although Marx did not really address crime specifically in his writing. Marxists emphasize that a class-based structure creates inequalities that will inevitably create tensions and conflict. Part of the focus of Marxist theory is on the preferential treatment that businesses and those in the upper class receive from the government and law. Marxist theory is in complete contrast with consensus theorists, who contend that the law is designed to maintain a fair and unbiased society and is based on the consensus of thought in a democratic society. By focusing on the government's role in crime and criminal justice, Marxist ideology undeniably provides the groundings for conflict theory.

In general, conflict theorists view crime as the outcome of a class struggle between the haves and have-nots in society. Those in power use the law and criminal justice system in a subtle manner that protects their interests. Crime and crime control methods serve to maintain the position of the haves and continue control over the have nots. Criminals are not necessarily seen as deficient. Rather, criminals may simply be responding to the inequality built into the system.[24]

During the 1970s (and to this day), conflict theorists could find a great deal of support for their contentions. White-collar crime is investigated, prosecuted, and sanctioned much less severely than those who commit lower-class crime. Similarly, conflict theorists contend that victims of crime who are wealthy and have influence receive quick reactions from criminal justice agents, whereas these same agents are often disinterested in crimes against the lower class.[25]

For the first time, theories developed in this time period addressed females specifically. The Liberation Hypothesis, proposed in 1975, posits that women will engage in crimes traditionally associated with males as they become more liberated. The Women's Movement of the 1970s was a tremendous influence on criminologists. Women's Movement reformers advanced new policies and new ways of thinking that challenged the androcentrism in theory and research of prior decades. Specifically, feminists maintained that the criminology of previous decades had involved male researchers who generally studied male subjects. Thus, they developed theories to explain male violence and delinquency that might not be applicable to female delinquency.[26]

Rita Simon was the first to offer a liberation perspective in her 1975 text, *Women and Crime.* Simon felt that women's greater participation in the workplace would lead to greater involvement in white-collar activities. She did not feel liberation would impact female involvement in violence crime. Although women may feel violent urges due to their exploitation and subservience in society, they would not be willing to submit to those urges because they would not want to jeopardize their new opportunities.[27]

In the same year, Freda Adler more clearly articulated the Liberation Hypothesis with the publication of her book, *Sisters in Crime: The Rise of the New Female Criminal*. Adler cited skyrocketing arrest statistics for a number of offenses to argue that women were engaging in not only more crime, but different types of crime. For instance, between 1960 and 1972, female arrests for burglary went up 168 percent. Arrests of females for robbery, embezzlement, and larceny increased 277 percent, 280 percent, and 300 percent, respectively. Adler was a harsh critic of prior criminological thought. First, it rarely addressed females at all. When they did include females, earlier criminological theories tended to presume women were hysterical, biological aberrations.[28]

SIGNIFICANT COURT CASES

There is still much debate regarding whether juveniles can truly comprehend, and thus should be able to waive, important constitutional rights. In *Miranda v. Arizona,* the Supreme Court held that police must inform people of their right against self-incrimination. *In re Gault* determined that constitutional guarantees of due process apply to juveniles, but did not clarify whether juveniles can waive Miranda rights. *Kent v. United States* also affirmed that juveniles are to receive due process, including being told their right to remain silent. Both *Kent* and *Breed v. Jones* established that juveniles must receive waiver hearings if they are to be tried in adult courts, and that trying them for the same offense in juvenile and adult court constituted double jeopardy.[29]

In the 1967 case *People v. Lara*, the California court held that the question of whether a juvenile can waive his or her Miranda rights must be decided by considering the totality of the circumstances. Factors to be considered include the age of the youth, his/her education, his/her understanding of the charge(s), the method of interrogation, and whether the individual was able to consult with family and friends. The court upheld the "totality of circumstances" standard in *Fare v. Michael*.[30] In *Fare*, the court held that asking to speak to a probation officer was not the same thing as asking to speak to an attorney, thus statements made to police were still admissible. In *California v. Prysock,* the court allowed a young man's waiver of Miranda rights even though the warning had been given in a slightly different language and out of context.[31]

Research seems to suggest that juvenile offenders, in particular those under the age of 15, do not adequately understand what it means to waive Miranda rights.[32] Others replicated Grisso's study and found similar results.[33] Many researchers have concluded that juveniles are simply not able to waive their rights in a knowing and intelligent manner, the standard for adults.

The Supreme Court has affirmed that adults facing incarceration must have legal representation (see *Scott v. Illinois* (440 U.S. 367)), but has not done so with juveniles. More than one-half of juvenile offenders in Minnesota in 1986, with half of those incarcerated in secure detention, did not have legal counsel.[34] Conversely, research seems to suggest that juveniles with counsel are given more severe sanctions. Prior to the *Gault* case, approximately 5 percent of the young people appearing in juvenile court had legal representation.[35]

In *McKeiver v. Pennsylvania* (403 U.S. 528 [1971]), the court relied on the notion of state as parent when they held that a jury trial is not required during delinquency proceedings. In *Breed v. Jones* (421 U.S. 519 [1975]), the Supreme Court held that the double jeopardy clause of the Fifth Amendment applies to juveniles. In 1975, the Supreme Court held that suspending or expelling a student without a hearing violates their Fifth Amendment right to due process (*Goss v. Lopez* (419 U.S. 565)).[36]

The Supreme Court dealt with the issue of search and seizure frequently in this time period. A notable case was *Mapp v. Ohio* in 1961, which established the exclusionary rule. The exclusionary rule prohibits material obtained from an illegal search from being used against a person in court. In 1967, the court extended the ban on unreasonable searches and seizures to juveniles, although it is unclear whether the exclusionary rule was allowed in juvenile court. Although these cases seem to extend important privacy protections to juveniles, other decisions made it easier to search young people. In 1985, in *New Jersey v. T.L.O.*, the court set the standard for school administrators searching juveniles. Rather than searches based on probable cause, which is required for police, administrators are authorized to search juveniles based on reasonable suspicion, a much lower standard.[37]

In the 1970s, courts dealt several times with issues of abuse in detention. In 1976 in *Pena v. New York State Division for Youth,* the court determined that use of isolation, hand restraints, and tranquilizing drugs was in violation of the Eighth Amendment prohibition against cruel and unusual punishment. In another case, *Inmates of the Boys Training School v. Affeck,* the court held that holding juveniles in cells, naked, was in violation of the Eighth Amendment.[38]

In opposition to the extension of rights afforded to juveniles by decisions in the 1960s and early 1970s, a series of decisions in the 1980s demonstrated the more punitive trend. Most notably, the court affirmed that using the death penalty with juveniles did not violate the Eighth Amendment. In 1989, the court determined juveniles age 16 or over can be executed in *Stanford v. Kentucky*. Twenty to 27 juveniles were executed each decade between the 1880s and 1920s. Juvenile executions reached a peak of 53 in the 1940s. Between 1977 and 1986, only three juveniles were actually executed.[39]

THE JUVENILE JUSTICE SYSTEM

Detaining Youth

One of the major concerns has always been the impact of incarceration on youth. One specific concern pertains to detaining youth prior to adjudication. In *United States v. Salerno* (481 U.S. 739 [1987]), the Supreme Court approved preventive detention for a specific list of offenses and in cases where clear and convincing evidence demonstrates a threat to public safety. In contrast, the court has upheld preventive detention of youth who pose a "serious risk" with no such regulations on offense type (*Schall v. Martin* (467 U.S. 283 [1984]).

Concerns about detaining youth are especially salient when applied to status offenders. Beginning in the 1960s, California led the movement to separate delinquents from status offenders.[40] Massachusetts led the way with deinstitutionalizing juvenile offenders in general. The Massachusetts Department of Youth Service closed the training schools for youth in 1970 and 1971, preceding other states by two decades.[41]

Even into the 1970s, courts upheld the incarceration of so-called stubborn children. In the 1970s, Arkansas allowed for county judges to commit children ages three to 15 who "live in notorious records of bad character." State laws dealing with juvenile status offenses tend to use derogatory language and to be very vague. For instance, Kansas called troubled children "miscreants," while others called young people evil, vicious, wicked, and depraved. In 1971, almost one-third of the juvenile court cases in Cook County, Illinois, were status offenders; in California, status offenses represented 56.4 percent of all juvenile arrests.[42]

The story of Stanley Eldridge highlights the problems with incarcerating low-level juvenile offenders. Eldridge was eight when he hid in his aunt's closet after running away and accidentally caught her clothes on fire. He was incarcerated for 13 years at Rikers Island. Eldridge described his experience with juvenile justice this way: "it didn't make sense to commit a petty crime. The judge usually gave you the maximum sentence out of contempt. No one bailed you out and fellow cons either ignored you or tolerated you.

So what you did was listen to the tales of bank jobs and felonious assaults and shootouts and write yourself a script and find out where to cop a piece when you hit the streets."[43]

The case of serial killer Charles Manson is illustrative of how a poor home life, in conjunction with early involvement in juvenile justice, can foster criminal activity. Manson's mother, Kathleen Maddox, was 16 when she gave birth, likely the result of being raped. Manson's birth certificate called him "No Name Maddox." When he was young, Charlie frequently was left with his grandmother and aunt because his mother would disappear for days and weeks at a time. In 1939, Maddox began a five-year sentence in the West Virginia State Penitentiary for armed robbery and Charlie stayed with an aunt. When Maddox was released Charlie returned to live with her and the revolving door of "uncles." They moved a lot, often staying in hotel rooms, and Charlie stayed by himself a lot. He also ran away frequently. For a brief stint he stayed with foster parents, but his mother moved to Indianapolis with a man and sent for Charlie. By 1947, Maddox wanted Charlie back in the foster system but no placement was available so he became a ward of the state. Charlie ran away from the Gibault Home for Boys in Terre Haute, Indiana and returned to his mother, who rejected him. He then began a life of crime. He was caught stealing a bike and was sent to a juvenile center, but escaped. Every time he was incarcerated, he tried to escape or run away. Ken Wooden visited the Gibault Home in the 1970s. He was shown the long, thick, leather straps used to "discipline" the boys. Records demonstrated Manson had been beaten so severely that he needed hospital attention on several occasions. Records also showed Manson was raped.[44]

In 1973 in Texas, state and federal courts mandated the release of more than 800 youth from penal facilities. At the heart of the massive litigation was the question of whether the juvenile correctional system is designed to punish, or to parent—that is, to rehabilitate and teach. The federal case *Morales v. Turman,* began when 15-year-old runaway Guadalupe Torres told attorney Steve Bercu she feared being locked up in a detention center. Upon investigation, Bercu learned that El Paso County had been sending a disproportionate number of youth to a detention facility. The youth were not afforded an attorney, and one-third of them never had any form of legal hearing. Most had committed status offenses. Bercu sought the release of all 75 of the youth from El Paso County held at the Gainesville State School and was granted a release to speak to the youth who had been incarcerated without a hearing. One of them was Alicia Morales.[45]

Morales, as well as nine others, testified in the spring of 1971 about cruel and unusual punishment at Gainesville State School, and federal judge Wayne

Justice mandated interviews of all the children incarcerated through the Texas Youth Council. He also ordered a team of social workers and psychologists to study two of the facilities. These interviews and observations led to involvement of the U.S. Department of Justice and the FBI. These federal representatives reported gross violations of basic civil rights and a failure to provide a rehabilitative environment.[46]

Testimony in *Morales v. Turner* showed that 24 percent of the 2,442 juveniles held by the Texas Youth Council (TYC) were there for disobedience, with many others being held for running away, truancy, and being "ungovernable." Less than 10 percent had committed an offense against a person. Abuse was justified by TYC employees by the Texas Corporal Punishment law, a vague statute that authorized whipping. Incarcerated youth described far more brutal abuse. One 14-year-old boy testified about "the peel," in which a guard would hit the back of the youth's head with the palm of his hand while he knelt with his head between the guard's legs. Also popular with guards were "running in place," "the tight," and "crumb." Running in place involved the guard running in place while the child's head was between their legs, causing painful burning and headaches from the friction. In the tight, the youth was forced to bend over and touch his toes while the guard beat him with a broomstick. Crumb was used on weekends. Youth were forced to face a wall or fence all day and stay awake but in complete silence, despite the fact that most received large does of the tranquilizer Thorazine that made them sleepy. Youth also reported being injured by dogs that chased them when they had run away. More than one-third of the boys at Gatesville ran away in one year.[47]

Boys were terribly afraid of being transferred to Mountain View, the maximum security facility allegedly built for hardcore offenders, and went to great lengths to avoid it. Some attempted suicide multiple times. In May 1972, 68 percent of the youth at Mountain View were first-time offenders, disproportionately minority, poor, and lacking education. Many had IQs in the retarded range. Testimony about the treatment at Mountain View was horrific. One retarded and epileptic boy was locked in solitary confinement while guards threw canisters of tear gas under the door. He clawed into the wall trying to escape. Gassing was relatively common. Further examination of facility records revealed no rhyme or reason to why youth were placed in solitary confinement. Some were sent for writing illegal letters, trying to make a long-distance phone call, and pretending to be sick. Fifteen were locked in solitary for a total of 357 days for trying to masturbate.[48]

Girls reported being beaten while handcuffed. One girl who arrived four months pregnant was given pills and made to exercise. The combination made her abort, but she received no medical attention until one month later. Although almost one-quarter of the girls spoke Spanish, they would be punished for doing so because the language was prohibited.[49]

When Judge Justice released his ruling about the abuse at TYC, riots broke out at some of the facilities. "The kids did what the courts could not and the state would not do. With their own hands they ripped out and destroyed the contents of those cells where countless numbers of them lived in daily fear of being beaten into submission."[50] As a result of the case, the dogs used to chase runaways were given up, and youth were no longer committed to the TYC for truancy, incorrigibility, or running away.[51]

In the 1970s, journalists began exposing the abuse at juvenile facilities across the country. No state was left untouched. In 1972 and 1973, the John Howard Association conducted interviews with 90 children from the Audy Home in Chicago. They heard horrifying stories of kids being hit, kicked and slapped, forced to endure the winter cold, drink from the toilet, and being sodomized by broomsticks. In Massachusetts, a Harvard undergraduate posed as a delinquent and witnessed guards holding children's heads in water and others using a child's head to mop urine from the floor. In one of the most horrifying stories, a Massachusetts boy defecated in the carrot shed after a guard would not let him go. Legal affidavits recorded the following testimony:

The guard grabbed the kid by the hair and dragged him to put his face in the shit. The kid refused. The guard grabbed him by the hair and collar, kicked him to his knees and stuck his face in the shit saying, "That'll teach you to shit in the carrot shed, you cock sucker." The kid got up and tried to wash his face off in the barn sink. Another guard was in the barn and wouldn't let the kid wash his face. Instead he hosed him down from head to foot.[52]

In Alabama, black children were sexually molested by guards and beaten with assorted implements.[53] In Virginia, two boys were ordered to kill a dog with a stick. In other locations, boredom is the primary punishment. In West Virginia, for instance, children were forced to sit at attention on a metal chair for six to eight hours a day, sometimes for three to six straight weeks, in complete silence.[54]

Another concern was about the quantity and quality of educational and other types of treatment programs available for youth. Ken Wooden assessed the reading level of incarcerated juveniles in 1974 and found the average reading ability to be fourth-grade level. He said his results echoed earlier ones from the 1920s, 1930s, and 1940s. What passed for education was often some canned educational machine or do-it-yourself booklet. In

1974, two federal district court judges (in Texas and Pennsylvania) ruled that incarcerated youth had the right to treatment, yet states still afforded few quality options. "What becomes obvious is the vicious cycle of virtual mental genocide committed against certain segments of the population by those who devise testing or promote its use."[55]

Florida has been the site of some of the most serious concerns about juvenile justice. In 1983, *Bobby M. v. Martinez* alleged that conditions in four institutions, housing more than 1,000 juveniles, were violating the inmates' civil rights. The suit alleged overcrowding, lack of security and discipline, inadequate medical and psychological care, cruel use of punishment and isolation, inappropriate placements, and inadequate education and rehabilitative programs. The suit resulted in a consent decree between the plaintiffs and the Department of Health and Rehabilitative Services (DHRS) requiring specialized treatment, establishment of assessment, classification and placement processes, increased community-based alternatives for nonviolent offenders, and programs to address high recidivism rates. The suit also required a cap on the population of youth in training schools to reduce overcrowding. Unfortunately, these conditions, in conjunction with the states broad transfer requirements, led to significant increases in the number of youths waived to adult courts. In 1982–1983, when the *Bobby M.* case was filed, there were 3,162 cases transferred. Between that year and 1987–1988, the number increased 22 percent, and then increased 65 percent between 1987–1988 and 1991–1992. Fewer than one-quarter were charged with a violent offense.[56]

Another concern in this era was about the appropriateness of using solitary confinement with young people. Research has repeatedly demonstrated that solitary confinement can be detrimental to a person's mental health. After a two-week period, people begin to lose visual skills and motor coordination and suffer from speech and hearing impairments. Solitary confinement also causes lethargy, and in many, depression.[57] The effects may be even worse on young people, as virtually all the research was conducted with adult samples. Interestingly, some states outlawed solitary confinement for adults but allowed it for juveniles, although in many cases it was called something else like "the control room."[58]

In lieu of, or sometimes in conjunction with, solitary confinement, facilities in the 1960s and 1970s use the tranquilizer Thorazine to subdue adult and juvenile inmates. Prolonged use of tranquilizers can cause liver and kidney damage, respiratory problems, bowel problems, and brain damage. Again, research about the damaging effects of Thorazine was conducted with adults, so it is unclear precisely what impact it has on juveniles.[59]

Disparity in the System

Another concern centers on disparity in the system. In the 1980s, researchers began to collect more systematic data on disparity based on race, socioeconomic status, and gender. Studies have repeatedly affirmed racial disparity in detention, even when offense-related variables are controlled.[60] Additionally, non-white youth are more likely to be placed in public correctional facilities, whereas white youth are overrepresented in privately run group homes, foster homes, and drug and alcohol treatment programs.[61]

A University of Chicago study in 1970 found more females locked up for status offenses than males, and that girls were generally incarcerated longer. Other studies around the nation echoed those findings.[62] Girls' prisons were also found to have far more security measures despite the relative harmlessness of their offenses. For instance, in Dade County, Florida, girls were kept in steel cages. In Colorado, girls were hog tied and left lying on the floor in isolation rooms far smaller than those for boys. Testimony from the previously mentioned trial of *Morales v. Turner* demonstrated that the nutrition in the girls' facility was so poor that over 80 percent of the girls suffered from nutrition-related skin disorders and required treatment. Girls in Texas were also forced to urinate in coke bottles for punishment, and a Monthly Menstruation Report hung on the door of females' cottages indicating the start and end of her period. Incarcerated girls were often subject to three or four pelvic exams. In Texas, a girl undergoing surgery for swallowing papers later found out she had been given a hysterectomy.[63]

Pregnant girls fared even worse. In Chicago, pregnant girls were often held in solitary confinement to punish them. In Texas, pregnant girls were given the choice of spending time in solitary confinement or aborting their babies.[64]

There were also concerns about treatment of those with mental health issues or learning disabilities. "Though these is little documentation on just how widespread the practice is, evidence exists that mentally retarded children in institutions are providing science and medicine, particularly the pharmaceutical industry, with highly suitable and unsuspecting or at least intimidated subjects for research."[65] For example, Pennsylvania had plans in the 1970s to test a new gonorrhea vaccine on mentally retarded children and Texas had given controversial birth control medication to 900 mentally retarded female inmates.[66]

Many people simply accepted that the juvenile justice system was what it said it was—a rehabilitative, nurturing environment.

An accurate perception of the juvenile court system is hidden by its euphemistic language. Confinement is commonly called "treatment" or "shelter care." A locked place of detention may be called a "group home." Training school confinement blocks are called "cottages." Cells in a detention center are called "bedrooms." Solitary confinement is called "quiet time." This modern double-speak explains many of the problems of the juvenile court, and it defeats reformers who are satisfied with words of promise from those who support its authority.[67]

NEW LEGISLATION

As noted in earlier chapters, juvenile justice has pretty much been left up to individual states. In the late 1960s and beyond, however, the federal government increasingly passed legislation requiring certain things from the states. The Juvenile Justice and Delinquency Prevention Act (JJDPA) of 1974 stipulated that juveniles could no longer be placed in any institution in which they may have regular contact with adults that have been convicted of criminal charges. The 1974 JJDPA also recommended juveniles be diverted from the justice system and into community-based programs. The JJDPA further provided for the deinstitutionalization of status offenders.[68] The 1974 JJDPA followed a string of lawsuits in many states about the conditions of confinement for youth. Most of the suits involved abuse by guards, excessive use of solitary confinement, and widespread distribution of Thorazine.[69] States that participated in the JJDPA (those wishing to receive any federal funds) were ordered to remove status offenders from secure detention and correctional facilities within two years. The JJDPA replaced the Juvenile Delinquency Prevention and Control Act (JDPCA) of 1968, which was responsible for the creation and implementation of juvenile delinquency plans for states that received federal funds. Deinstitutionalization proved more difficult than it sounds, as in many cases status offenders had committed other offenses as well.[70] Many Youth Service Bureaus (YSBs) were created from federal funds to assist in diverting youth from the formal juvenile justice system. These Bureaus provided counseling, job training, education, and recreational opportunities for youth.[71] Seemingly a good idea, diversion too had (and has) its critics. Now, young people whose behavior might previously have garnered a warning by law enforcement were moved into diversion programs, a phenomenon called net widening.

The JJDPA was authorized for three years with a budget of $350 million. Discretionary funds were used to support programs developed by public and private agencies for America's youth.[72] The JJDPA also created a National

Advisory Committee, a Federal Coordinating Council, and the National Institute for Juvenile Justice and Delinquency Prevention.

It would seem logical to believe that the mandated diversion and desinstitutionalization required by the JJDPA would benefit young ladies significantly, because they were the largest number of status offenders. In reality, however, "instead of being *de*institutionalized, girls [were] *trans*institutionalized into mental health facilities for behaviors labeled 'inappropriate' since the early decades of the juvenile court."[73]

The Juvenile Justice Act of 1977 established rules pertaining to procedures in the juvenile justice system. Under this act, the juvenile court system added some of the procedural methods commonly found in the adult system. It also attempted to address the concern about young people's understanding of procedural and constitutional rights.

The JJDPA also changed the personnel responsible for certain procedures in the juvenile courts. Prosecutors instead of probation officers were now responsible for charging decisions based on the juvenile's prior record and the strength of the particular case. Moreover, juveniles were now allowed a hearing to determine whether the accusation for which they were facing was accurate.[74]

CONCLUSIONS AND EMERGING ALTERNATIVES

The problems with juvenile justice were repeatedly exposed in this era, and challenges to many of the practices were addressed in the courts. Still, many held on to the idea that the juvenile justice system was the best way to deal with juvenile violence, but that the system simply needed some work. Others maintained that we should look outside the juvenile justice system for a more comprehensive approach with youth.

Building on the work of Cloward and Ohlin (described in Chapter 5), the New York City Mobilization for Youth (MOBY) program was intended to be an integrated approach to community development. The idea was to provide legitimate opportunities for economic and social success in communities where these were lacking. More than that, MOBY was supposed to move residents to action. MOBY leaders helped organize boycotts against schools, rent strikes against landlords, lawsuits seeking civil rights, and voter registration programs.[75] Funded by the federal government for $50 million, MOBY ended amidst claims it was doing nothing but draining the federal coffers.[76]

Another federally funded program that emerged in the 1960s was intended to address delinquency by providing educational opportunities to young children. Head Start began as a summer program with the philosophy to embrace the "whole child," so the program included traditional educational concepts as well as social skills, physical health, and emotional and mental health. In addition, staff visit parents at their homes to help them learn parenting skills. Head Start is still in operation today as a school readiness program. Research has found it to increase children's IQs, decrease the likelihood of later grade retention, and increase graduation rates. Additionally, Head Start kids have better health and nutrition, immunization rates, and score higher on social competence scales than do similar students who do not attend.[77]

In the late 1980s, Massachusetts Commissioner of Public Health Deborah Prothrow-Stith called for a public health approach to juvenile violence. Rather than treating youth violence as solely a criminal or juvenile justice concern, Prothrow-Stith maintained that because violence destroys so many lives, it must be handled with a more comprehensive approach. She maintained that emergency rooms could be a prominent location for outreach.[78] These and other alternatives set the stage for the emergence of new ideas and programs for delinquent youth.

NOTES

1. Bartollas, C., & Miller, S. (1994). *Juvenile justice in America.* New York: Pearson, p. 4.

2. Bernard, T. (1999). Juvenile crime and the transformation of juvenile justice: Is there a juvenile crime wave? *Justice Quarterly, 16*(2), 337–356.

3. Guarino-Ghezzi, S., & Loughran, E. (2004). *Balancing juvenile justice.* New Brunswick, NJ: Transaction Publishers.

4. Bartolas & Miller (1994).

5. Feld, B. (2005). Race and the jurisprudence of juvenile justice: A tale in two parts, 1950–2000. In D. Hawkins (Ed.). *Our children, their children* (pp. 122–163). Chicago, IL: University of Chicago Press.

6. Aloisi, M. (2004). Emerging trends and issues in juvenile justice. In B. Hancock & P. Sharp (Eds.). *Public policy, crime, and criminal justice* (3rd ed., pp. 350–364). Upper Saddle River, NJ: Prentice Hall.

7. McCord, J. (1978). A thirty-year follow-up of treatment effects. *American Psychologist, 33,* 284–89.

8. Parenti, C. (1999). *Lockdown America.* London: Verso, p. 7.

9. Krisberg, B. (1998). The evolution of an American institution. *Crime and Delinquency 44,* 1–5.

10. Benekos, P., & Merlo, A. (2002). Reaffirming juvenile justice. In R. Muraskin & A. Roberts (Eds). *Visions for change* (3rd ed., pp. 265–286). Upper Saddle River, NJ: Prentice Hall.

11. Katz, M. (1986). *In the shadow of the poorhouse: A social history of welfare in America.* New York: Basic.

12. Guarino-Ghezzi & Loughran (2004).

13. Feld (2005).

14. Zimring, F. (1997). *Crime is not the problem: Lethal violence in America.* New York: Oxford University Press.

15. Snyder, H., & Sickmund, M. (1999). *Juvenile offenders and victims: 1999 National Report.* Office of Juvenile Justice and Delinquency Prevention.

16. Hancock, L. (2003). Wolfpack: The press and the Central park Jogger. *Columbia Journalism Review, 38,* 38–42.

17. Aloisi (2004).

18. Parenti (1999).

19. Ibid.

20. Sherman (2006, January 17). City seeks to widen sex-offender limits. *The Miami Herald,* p. 1–2B.

21. Hirschi, T. (1969). *Causes of delinquency.* Berkeley, CA: University of California Press.

22. Becker, H. (1973). *Outsiders: Studies in the sociology of deviance.* New York: The Free Press.

23. Schmalleger (2005). *Criminology today* (3rd ed.). Upper Saddle River, NJ: Prentice Hall.

24. Ibid.

25. Ibid.

26. Adler, F. (1975). *Sisters in crime: The rise of the new female criminal.* New York: McGraw-Hill.

27. Ibid.

28. Ibid.

29. Lawrence, R. (1998). *School crime and juvenile justice.* New York: Oxford University Press.

30. Ibid.

31. Siegel, L., Welsh, B., & Senna, J. (2003). *Juvenile delinquency, eighth edition.* Belmont, CA: Wadsworth.

32. Grisso, T. (1981). *Juveniles' waiver of rights: Legal and psychological competence.* New York: Plenum.

33. Lawrence, R. (1983). The role of legal counsel in juveniles' understanding of their rights. *Juvenile and Family Court Journal, 34*(4), 49–58.

34. Feld (1999).

35. Feld (1989).

36. Feld (2005).

37. Finley, L., & Finley, P. (2005). *Piss off!* Monroe, ME: Common Courage Press.

38. Wooden, K. (2000). *Weeping in the playtime of others* (2nd ed.). Columbus, OH: Ohio State University Press.

39. Bartolas & Miller (1994).

40. Wooden (2000).

41. Guarino-Ghezzi & Loughran (2004).

42. Wooden (2000).

43. Ibid., p. 41.

44. Ibid.

45. Ibid.

46. Ibid.

47. Ibid.

48. Ibid.

49. Ibid.

50. Ibid., p. 18.

51. Ibid.

52. Ibid., p. 113.

53. Ibid.

54. Ibid., p. 113.

55. Ibid., p. 61.

56. Guarino-Ghezzi & Loughran (2004).

57. Wooden (2000).

58. Ibid.

59. Ibid.

60. See Bishop, D., & Frazier, C. (1988). The influence of race in juvenile justice processing. *Journal of Research in Crime and Delinquency, 25,* 242–263; Kempf, K., Decker, S., & Bing, R. (1990). *An analysis of apparent disparities in the handling of Black youth within Missouri's juvenile justice systems.* St. Louis: Department of Administration of Justice, University of Missouri-St. Louis; Secret, P., & Johnson, J. (1997). The effects of race on juvenile justice decision-making in Nebraska: Detention, adjudication, and disposition, 1988–1993. *Justice Quarterly, 14,* 445–578.

61. Bishop, D. (2005). Race and ethnicity in processing. In D. Hawkins & K. Kempf-Leonard (Eds.). *Our children, their children* (pp. 23–82). Chicago, IL: University of Chicago Press.

62. Wooden (2000).

63. Ibid.

64. Ibid.

65. Ibid., p. 75.

66. Ibid.

67. Orlando, F., & Crippen, G. (1994). The rights of children and the juvenile court. Schwartz, I. (Ed.). *Juvenile justice and public policy: Toward a national agenda* (pp. 89–100). New York: Lexington, p. 96.

68. Kobrin, S., & Klein, M. (1982). *National evaluation of the deinstitutionalization of status offender programs: Executive summary.* Washington, DC: U.S. Department of Justice.

69. Guarino-Ghezzi & Loughran (2004).

70. Kobrin & Klein (1982).

71. Lawrence (1998).

72. The Juvenile Justice and Delinquency Prevention Act of 1974 (n.d.). Available at: http://www.ncjrs.org/

73. Federle, K., & Chesney-Lind, M. (1994). Special issues in juvenile justice: Gender, race, and ethnicity. In I. Schwartz (Ed.). *Juvenile justice and public policy: Toward a national agenda* (pp. 165–195). New York: Lexington, p. 165.

74. Krisberg, B. (1998). The evolution of an American institution. *Crime and Delinquency,* 44, 1–5.

75. Schmalleger (2005).

76. Siegel et al. (2003).

77. Zigler, E & Styfko, S. (1994). Head Start, criticisms in a constructive context. *American Psychologist, 49,* 127–132.

78. Prothrow-Stith, D. (1991). *Deadly consequences.* New York: HarperPerennial.

6

1990s through 2000

INTRODUCTION

The "get tough" approach to juvenile justice that emerged in the 1970s and 1980s persisted in the 1990s, despite evidence that juvenile crime decreased. The 1990s saw, in contrast to predictions, decreases in many types of juvenile crime. Most notably, arrests for index crimes, including murder, forcible rape, robbery, and aggravated assault declined 3 percent in 1995.[1] For the eighth year in a row, overall crime rates were down in 1999. Between 1993 and 1997, the arrest rate for juveniles decreased 39 percent.[2] Less than 1 percent of all juveniles in the nation are ever arrested for a violent crime.[3]

Fear of the juvenile superpredator was not just an attitude. Rather, this fear prompted policy initiatives. As in the 1980s, many considered it political suicide to argue for more nurturing or rehabilitative approaches to juvenile justice. Educators Hyman and Snook summed it up nicely:

If you are a politician and you really want to get elected in America, get tough on crime. It doesn't matter that crime is actually decreasing, conservative candidates for office believe that if you scare the hell out of voters, you will get their vote. Slogans associated with this strategy include "zero tolerance," "just say no," and "three strikes you're out." Of course few politicians consider how these slogans may affect innocent students.[4]

Get-tough attitudes were clear from the titles and provisions of legislation and programs. For instance, in 1989, California passed a law authorizing the arrest of parents who failed to control their children's delinquency. Parents could be subject to incarceration as well as a $2,500 fine.[5] Schools across the nation adopted "zero tolerance" policies for a variety of disciplinary infractions in the mid 1990s. In 1994, Congress enacted the Violent Crime Control and Law Enforcement Act. It authorized greater expenditures on policing, funds for building more prisons, expanded use of the federal death penalty, and efforts to increase border control. Additionally, it increased penalties for making or dealing drugs near schools.[6] In New York City, police commissioner William Bratton, following the lead of Mayor Rudy Giuliani, implemented zero tolerance policing, also called "quality of life" policing. The idea was that crackdowns on the "social junk," those people who commit low-level public order offenses, would prevent more serious incidents.[7] "Three strikes and you're out" legislation swept quickly across the nation in the wake of the heavily publicized murder of Polly Klaas in California. Although largely targeted at adult offenders, people under the age of 20 were also sentenced under the new legislation. A bill introduced into the House of Representatives that would have dramatically revamped the juvenile justice system was originally titled the Violent Youth Predator Act.[8]

In fact, "new" types of offenses, such as school shootings, furthered the get-tough mentality. Although violence in schools was by no means new, nor was it necessarily worse than in previous eras, media attention prompted a moral panic about school violence. Moral panics typically incite calls for serious and punitive approaches.[9] As noted in Chapter 6, well-known academics, practitioners, politicians, and pundits announced the coming of the superpredator juvenile. These hyperviolent thugs were supposedly running amok, and the most severe sanctions were required in response. Curfew laws for juveniles, expanded use of waivers to adult courts and minimum sentences, and school-based zero tolerance laws are all examined in this chapter.

It is critical to mention the disjuncture between beliefs about juvenile crime and reality. Mike Males said this about the prediction of the wave of superpredators: "It is difficult to imagine a prediction that turned out to be more monumentally wrong."[10] Males examined the increase in felony crime in California between 1980 and 1997. He found that, rather than young people, white adults over the age of 30 were responsible for the largest increases. For instance, while violent crime by 10 to 19-year-olds increased 6 percent in the time period, among 20–29-year-olds it increases 47 percent and among those over 30, there was a whopping 148 percent increase. For nonwhite youths, felony arrests decreased 32 percent between 1976 and 1997.[11]

At the same time, other researchers and practitioners continued to examine alternatives to formal juvenile justice. Additionally, there were seeds of more therapeutic approaches within the system. As always, some states were more progressive than others and explored these alternatives. Some of these alternatives will be detailed in this chapter. New and updated theories aided in the understanding of the gendered nature of offending as well as how offending plays out over the life course. These theories supported changes in some legal policies, such as use of the death penalty, and programs. Innovations included diverting youth to community-based programs, coordinated, multipurpose interventions in specific communities, and even complete overhauls of juvenile justice philosophy and systems.

For instance, during the late 1990s, activists attempted to mobilize their communities to fix the numerous problems they perceived in the juvenile justice system. Groups such as the Maryland Juvenile Justice Coalition, the Juvenile Justice Project of Louisiana, the Prison Moratorium Project and the Justice 4 Youth Coalition in New York, and California's Books Not Bars are examples of grassroots activists.

Activities by these and other groups brought attention to the atrocities in America's youth detention centers, such as the Tallulah correctional facility in Louisiana, the Cheltenham and Hickey facilities in Maryland, New York City's Spofford detention center, and the California Youth Authority. All of these institutions were known for their high incidences of violence. In fact Human Rights Watch, an international human rights organization, investigated the harsh conditions and violence in Tallulah. The U.S. Justice Department also opened investigations of Tallulah and both of the Maryland facilities, and investigated physical, mental, and sexual abuses in over 85 other juvenile detention centers.

It is unclear precisely what caused the decrease in juvenile violence in the 1990s. What is clear is that everyone wanted credit for the decline. Conservatives maintained their get-tough initiatives were paying off, and more of the same was needed to continue the decrease. Others contended that these efforts had no impact. Rather, the decrease was a result of innovative approaches and a vibrant economy.

NEW THEORIES

Developmental theories emphasize the age a juvenile begins offending as a critical variable in explaining their persistent delinquency. Research supports the fact that the most serious adult offenders began offending very early, even at pre-school age. These offenders tend to exhibit a variety of antisocial behavior, including truancy, animal cruelty, lying, and theft. One study found males who begin offending prior to the age of 14 were most likely to engage in serious offending by age 18. The most serious offenders had exhibited antisocial behavior at the youngest ages.

There are a variety of different developmental theories. Some developmental theories stress the influence of important events, or life transitions, as pivotal points in an individual's path to either offending or persistence. Important transitions include completing education, leaving the parents' home, entering the workforce in a career, finding permanent relationships, marrying, and beginning their own family. These are supposed to occur in succession. When transitions occur too early or too late, delinquency may result. For instance, teens that drop out of school are at greater risk for continued delinquency. Because some people are more at risk than others, they are more susceptible to offending when a transition is disrupted. Impoverished African American males are more likely to drop out of school. They are also more likely to be on the receiving end of discriminatory policing. Out of school and profiled by the police, they are more likely to engage in and be caught for delinquent activity. On the reverse, positive transitions can help an individual cease being delinquent. Students who graduate and move on to college, work, or military service often desist from offending. These theories suggest that early interventions and enhanced opportunities for young people can prevent adolescent offenders from escalating their involvement in crime.[12]

Rolf Loeber and associates used longitudinal data to develop three distinct paths to adult offending: authority conflict, covert, and overt. In the authority-conflict path, stubborn behavior at an early age may cause an individual to become defiant or disobedient. That individual may then learn to avoid authority, doing such things as staying out late, running away, and skipping school. The covert pathway begins with minor devious behavior, such as lying and shoplifting. These then escalate to more significant property damage, which escalates to more serious criminality, such as stealing cars, dealing drugs, and breaking and entering. In the overt pathway, individuals begin by exhibiting aggressive behavior, such as annoying others or bullying peers. They next engage in more serious physical altercations, and then to criminal acts of violence such as robbery and assault. Loeber and colleagues emphasized that the individuals who enter more than one pathway are the most persistent offenders. Again, the idea is that early identification of and intervention with a juvenile who has headed down one path is critical.[13]

Terrie Moffitt posited that, for most people, antisocial behavior peaks in adolescence. She calls these people *adolescent limiteds* (AL). These offenders generally engage in minor forms of delinquency that are generally considered typical of teenagers. For others, called *life-course persisters* (LC), offending continues into adulthood. Moffitt maintained that the combination of family dysfunction and neurological problems makes some offenders persist. Poor parenting prior to age 14 leads these individuals to commit deviant behaviors. They also become involved with delinquent peer groups, who reinforce the deviant behavior. Those who start their delinquent behavior after the age of 14 follow a slightly different path. First, they become involved with delinquent peers, who then lead them to delinquent involvement. There are different personal characteristics of the two types of offenders. Life-course persisters tend to have limited verbal ability, which often impacts their success in school. They seem to mature faster, and thus are more prone to early sexual involvement and drug use that might increase the likelihood of criminal involvement. Whereas adolescent limiteds focus mostly on one form of misbehavior, such as drug abuse or shoplifting, life-course persisters tend to engage in a variety of deviant behaviors.[14] More recently, Moffitt has adapted her theory to explain that some AL offenders may persist into adulthood if certain "snares," such as drug dependency or failure to complete an education, are present.[15]

In 1988, Jack Katz published his book, *Seductions of Crime.* In the book, Katz attempted to get inside the heads of delinquents and criminals in order to see what motivated them. Critical of purely sociological theories, Katz argued that delinquents choose to offend because it fulfills their need to take risks and obtain thrills.[16] Katz's ideas echoed those of much of the public— that delinquents chose to offend and actually enjoyed it. The implications of his research are huge. If juveniles do elect to offend because they find it pleasurable, it is critical to find alternative, legitimate ways for them to experience these thrills. Unfortunately, many respond to this type of theory with calls for more punitive approaches. If juveniles enjoy offending and are not remorseful, the thinking goes, then the harshest sentences are required.

In 1990, Gottfredson and Hirschi proposed their General Theory of Crime, another type of developmental theory. Rather than life events, however, Gottfredson and Hirschi maintained that the aging process explained the decreases in offending over time. Drawing on rational choice and routine activities theories, Gottfredson and Hirschi posited that delinquency is both rational and predictable. Offenders weigh the costs and benefits of their actions and decide to do that which they perceive as being advantageous.[17]

Gottfredson and Hirschi maintained that some delinquents are predisposed to offend. Although these juveniles are not constantly offending, when an opportunity for delinquency arises, these individuals are more prone to do so. They proposed that individual's propensity to be delinquent remains stable throughout their lifetime and it is the opportunities to offend that change.[18]

Gottfredson and Hirschi asserted that self-control is the key trait that makes one prone to delinquency. Those with limited self-control are more impulsive and adventuresome, tend to be physical risk takers and be active physically, are often insensitive to the feelings of others, are shortsighted, and often do not have well-developed communication skills. Further, they tend to lack perseverance. They often feel little shame when they engage in various forms of delinquency, instead finding them pleasurable. As these individuals get older, they are more likely to be involved in dangerous behaviors, such as drinking, reckless driving, and smoking, and they tend to have unstable work patterns and relationships. Basically, these individuals seek short-term gratification.[19]

People are not born with low self-control, according to Gottfredson and Hirschi. Rather, self-control is developed through socialization. The root cause of inadequate self-control is poor childrearing, according to Gottfredson and Hirschi. Parents might be inadequate in a number of ways. They might fail to or do a poor job of monitoring their child's behavior. They may not punish deviant behavior when it occurs; in fact, many parents do not even recognize deviant behavior in their children. In addition to families, schools are a key source for the development (or lack thereof) of self-control. Further, individuals with low self-control are prone to seek peers who also lack self-control.[20]

John Hagan's Power Control theory mixes elements of conflict, control, and feminist theories. Hagan contended that criminal behavior is highly influenced by family structure. Family structure reflects the patriarchal nature of the greater society.

According to the theory, individuals, especially juveniles, are products of various levels of control that are exercised by their families. In his analysis, Hagan differentiates between two types of family patterns—patriarchal and egalitarian. Patriarchal families are traditional and assume that males and females have separate and unequal roles and functions. The adult male is positioned in the family as the undisputed head of the household. He is the provider. Adult females are in subservient roles, and are concerned primarily with the family, reproduction, and household concerns. In egalitarian families, which have become more prevalent only in recent decades, there is a general sharing of familial responsibilities, a narrowing of the division of labor based on gender status, and less emphasis placed on specific gender roles. Patriarchal families are still the norm in most modern societies, while egalitarian families are less common.[21]

In Hagan's theory, families control boys differently than girls. This is especially true in patriarchal families. Parents exert less control on boys, whereas the actions of girls are far more limited. Due to more direct and consistent contact with the children, it is normally mothers, rather than fathers, who apply the controls and perpetuate the ideology of the separate spheres for males and females. Borrowing a typology from social psychologist Carol Gilligan, Hagan stated that the two types of control exerted on children are either relational (referring to control measures that involve affective or relationship ties) or instrumental (referring to control strategies that involve surveillance and restrictions on freedom). Patriarchal families will have higher rates of male delinquency due to the relative freedom allowed boys, and lower rates of female delinquency due to higher levels of social constraint from their families. This system of patriarchal families has traditionally been the case in Western society. As social changes have developed in which married women are now more prevalent in the occupational sphere, an egalitarian structure has emerged in some families and in these families, it is expected that there will be less differentiation in male and female delinquency rates. It is due to this greater level of freedom for girls that they will experience similar risk factors, resulting in higher delinquency rates for girls.[22]

Hagan conceptualizes three levels at which the patriarchal and egalitarian gender configurations apply. The first involves the micro level or social-psychological process that accounts for the specific juvenile behavior. The second level refers to the social positions within the family. The last level is the class structure in which families are organized. This is based on broader structural configurations that are patriarchal as well.

Hagan tested his theory in Canada and found empirical support. Other researchers have tested the Power Control theory but have obtained mixed results. Hagan's theory helps explain the concern about increased delinquency rates among females in the 1980s and 1990s. On the other hand, it also serves as a reminder that, throughout history, males have committed the vast majority of violent offenses and this is likely due to the way we socialize males and females.[23]

The 1990s saw renewed interest in the Liberation Hypothesis. As they did in the 1970s, academics cited statistics showing rapidly growing arrests for females. They determined that females were offending like males. Between 1978 and 1988, female arrests for violent crime increased 41.5 percent. Department of Justice statistics showed the violent crime rate for women more than doubled between 1987 and 1994. Arrests for girls for all violent crimes grew 12 percent between 1992 and 2001, with the biggest increase (23.5 percent), in arrests for aggravated assault. Deborah Prothrow-Stith, Professor of Public Health at Harvard University, pointed to the increasing number of violent females in videogames and movies, such as the character Lara Croft in the video and film, *Tomb Raider*. Further, Prothrow-Stith speculated that, "we have socialized girls to solve problems like boys."[24]

The Liberation Hypothesis became one of the media's favorites in the 1990s, regardless of whether the factual evidence truly suggests females were offending like males. The main focus was on females' increased involvement in gangs, stressing not only that girls were joining in record numbers, but that they, like their male counterparts, were committing violence in their involvement. In 1992, CBS aired an episode called "Girls in the Hood" on its' program, *Street Smarts*. The program began with a voiceover announcing, "Some of the politicians like to call it this the Year of the Woman. The women you are about to meet probably aren't what they had in mind. These women are active, they're independent, and they're exercising power in a field dominated by men."[25] In addition, these female gang members supposedly joined and committed violence not out of need, but out of desire to own fancy things. As in the 1970s, conservatives pointed the finger at women's liberation.

RENEWED INTEREST IN THE MEDIA

Concerns about the media's impact on juvenile delinquency re-emerged as a major issue in the 1980s, after a quieter period in the 1960s and 1970s. In particular, the gangster rap of black artists NWA (Niggas With Attitudes) and Ice-T elicited strong responses. When Ice-T released his single "Cop Killer," various advocacy groups pressured for more control over the lyrics and images available to young people. There is some evidence that violent music has been influential. For instance, 144 law enforcement officers were shot on duty in 1992. Interviews with the killers revealed that violent music, such as Ice-T's "Cop Killer," made them feel power and gave them a sense of purpose.[26] Some were reported to have sung this and other violent, anti-police songs at the police station when they were arrested. In the mid 1990s, several rappers were involved in various ways with homicide investigations, including popular artist Tupac Shakur, who was murdered in 1996.[27] Later, a 17-year-old was charged with stabbing a 14-year-old girl in front of a satanic altar he had built. He reportedly had been watching a Marilyn Manson video with a similar altar.

Looking to the media as not just a reporter but a source of delinquency hit an all new level in this time period. Following his conviction in October 1998, the families of the girls Michael Carneal killed filed a $33 million lawsuit against Carneal, his family, the school, the students who failed to report him, and several media companies, including AOL Time Warner, Nintendo, and Sega. The families alleged that Carneal's parents, his classmates, and the school knew Carneal was dangerous and failed to take action to prevent the shootings. They also blamed the entertainment industry for inciting Carneal's violent behavior. All of the cases, with the exception of that against Carneal, were dismissed before trial. In August 2000, Carneal entered a settlement with the families for $42 million, an amount the parents of the slain girls are unlikely ever to see.[28]

Images of violent youth in the decade many times fed racial stereotypes. For instance, films like *Boyz 'n the Hood* (1991), *Juice* (1992), *Menace II Society* (1993), and *Mi Vida Loca / My Crazy Life* (1993) depicted African American and Latino youth committing drive-by shootings, easily acquiring drugs, and privileging respect as their dominant value. Although some applauded these films as portraying the issues for youth in urban communities realistically, others said they simply reinforced misconceptions and stereotypes.[29] Michael Moore examined this notion in *Bowling for Columbine,* where he pokes fun at the popular show *Cops* for featuring mostly Black offenders. "The politicization of crime policies and the connection in the public and political minds between race and youth crime provided a powerful political incentive for changes in waiver policies that de-emphasized youths' 'amenability to treatment' and instead focused almost exclusively on 'public safety'."[30] These images emphasized the few, or the isolated incident, without examining the actual trends.

During the last quarter of the twentieth century there was a tendency to generalize about young people's well-being on the basis of certain horrific but isolated events. The literary term *synecdoche*—confusing a part for a whole—is helpful in understanding how late twentieth-century Americans constructed an image of youth in crisis, as shocking episodes reinforced an impression that childhood was disintegrating.[31]

Media coverage of school violence exacerbated the moral panic about juvenile delinquency. A poll of 1004 adults taken shortly after the Jonesboro shooting found 71 percent believed that a similar shooting in their town was either "likely" or "very likely." A similar poll taken three days after the Columbine shooting in 1999 found 80 percent of adults believed a shooting was likely or very likely in their community.[32] Harsh times call for harsh punishments. Politicians and pundits called for arming teachers, for greater surveillance in schools, for more metal detectors and similar technology, and for more officers on campus.

At the same time, vocal critics denounced the tendency to blame the media. In *Bowling for Columbine,* Michael Moore examined the violent media in the United States as a possible causal agent to violent crime in general and school violence specifically. Although he recognized that the media plays a role, he asserted it was in the form of sensationalization. Rather than prompt people to offend, the film suggested the primary effect of media is to induce fear and prompt harsh responses. An interview with shock musician Marilyn Manson is particularly insightful. Manson argued that all the focus on how his and other artists' work leads to violence simply defused attention from the broader social trends that are really to blame.

ISSUES IN THE JUVENILE COURTS

Because juvenile justice was intended to meet the particular needs of the offender, judges historically had a wide array of dispositions available. In the late 1980s and 1990s, the perception that juvenile violence was out of control prompted three changes that significantly limited those dispositional options. Blended adult and juvenile sentences, mandatory sentences, and the extension of juvenile court dispositional options beyond the age of 21 are all practices more consistent with the philosophy in the adult criminal justice system than in juvenile justice.[33]

Lobbying for harsher punishments continued into the later 1990s. In 1997, Congress considered the Violent and Repeat Juvenile Offender Act. It included: allowing teenagers accused of certain specified offenses to be housed with adult offenders indefinitely; incarcerating status offenders with adults for 24 hours or longer on weekends and holidays; allowing colleges access to juvenile arrest records (even if the arrest did not lead to conviction); requiring states to expel students for up to six months for regular use of tobacco; and giving prosecutors sole discretion in the use of waivers to adult court.[34] Perhaps the most significant example of the punitive trend in juvenile justice is the huge number of juvenile cases transferred to adult court.

Waivers to Adult Court

In 1978, New York led the charge of states trying juveniles as adults after 14-year-old Willie Bosket killed two men on the subway and bragged that nothing could be done to him because of his age. Between 1992 and 1995, 48 states made it easier to try juveniles as adults.[35] By the end of the 1990s, every state except Nevada had made it easier to try juveniles as adults.[36] In 1994, the Juvenile Justice Reform Act gave prosecutors the right to determine if a youth should be tried in adult court, and provided for transfer of first-time offenders in specific cases.[37]

There are three ways juveniles can be transferred to adult courts. Judicial waivers allow judges to make the decision, based on whether they perceive the juvenile to be amenable to rehabilitation. With prosecutorial discretion, the prosecutor makes the decision. This is also known as direct file.[38] States with automatic transfer (also called legislative exclusion or mandatory waiver laws) provide for juveniles to be waived to adult courts for specified crimes. Some states tie waiver decisions to the age of the offender, whereas others do not. As of 1999, there were 20 states with no minimum age for waiver.[39] According to the OJJDP, in 2002, children as young as 12 can be tried as adults in Colorado and Missouri, and in Kansas and Vermont, waivers are provided for children as young as age 10.[40]

Fifteen states have mandatory waiver laws, which require that specific cases be shifted to the adult courts. In 29 states, specific offenses, offenders, or both are eligible for this type of transfer. Typical excluded offenses are murder and violent crimes against the person, but in Alaska, Florida, Idaho, Montana, Vermont, and Washington youth charged with other felonies like burglary and who have previous felony adjudications can be automatically transferred as well.[41]

The most controversial form of transfer is prosecutorial waiver because prosecutors have all the discretion. Fourteen states plus Washington, DC use this method. There are two types of judicial waiver. In ordinary judicial waiver proceedings, the prosecutor must prove to the juvenile court judge that the case merits transfer. In presumptive judicial waiver, the defense bears the burden of proof.[42]

Fifteen states are using blended sentences, in which they combine procedures and punishments from the adult and juvenile systems.[43] The specifics of blended sentence models vary across states, but the crux is that they provide for more severe sanctions. In general, they allow juveniles who have been adjudicated in the juvenile justice system to be sentenced in the adult system.[44] In 25 states, juveniles in adult courts can petition for reverse waiver, or decertification, where they can maintain that their cases belong back in the juvenile court. Thirty-four states have "once an adult, always an adult" laws that state that juveniles previously prosecuted as adults must be prosecuted in adult courts for all subsequent charges. In some states this legislation only applies to subsequent felonies and in others the offender must be at least age 16.[45]

Precise figures on the number of juvenile offenders transferred to adult courts are unknown, but it is clear that the number grew between 1985 and 1994. The number of youth under the age of 16 waived to adult courts doubled in that time period.[46] Use has diminished somewhat since 1994. Between 1985 and 1997, there was a 118 percent increase in the number of juveniles convicted as adults and sent to prison.[47] There were 7,500 judicial waivers in 1999. Some states transfer youth more frequently than others, and estimates are that the number of prosecutorial waivers doubles or triples the number of judicial waivers annually.[48] Florida led the nation in transferring juveniles to adult prisons in 1999. In 2002, 1,518 young people were sent to Florida prisons for crimes committed when they were under 18.[49] According to research published in 2005, Florida transfers approximately 5,000 offenders each year through prosecutorial waivers.[50]

One of the most highly profiled examples of waiver policies in action was the case of Nathaniel Abraham. In 1997, at age 11, Nathaniel Abraham shot and killed Ronnie Green. Abraham was the youngest offender in the modern era to face murder charges as an adult, as a new Michigan law allowed for the transfer of juveniles for serious and violent offenses.[51] Abraham was sentenced to seven years in a maximum security juvenile detention center.[52]

Studies have been mixed regarding whether waiving youth to adult courts is a specific deterrent. Several have found waived youth are more likely to recidivate. For instance, Fagan compared recidivism rates for juveniles charged with first- and second-degree felonies in New York and New Jersey. Using matched pairs, he examined samples that were similar in all respects except for the way their cases were handled. He found that for some offenses, there was no relationship between jurisdiction and recidivism, but for others, juveniles treated in the adult system had greater recidivism rates. He concluded, "rather than affording greater community protection, the higher recidivism rates for the criminal court cohort suggest that public safety was, in fact, compromised by adjudication in the criminal court." [53] A 1996 study from Florida found that youth who were transferred to adult prisons were rearrested more often after release, and their re-arrests were for more serious, violent crimes. At the time, Florida waived more juveniles to adult court than all other states combined.[54] Studies in New York and New Jersey found recidivism rates for waived juveniles to be 29 percent higher than for juveniles kept in the juvenile system.[55]

Interestingly, sometimes juveniles receive lengthier sentences in the juvenile court system than in the adult court system. This is partly because adult jurors may be hesitant to assign more severe sanctions to young people. Further, the juvenile court tends to move more swiftly. The Coalition for Juvenile Justice reported in 1997 that the average time between arrest and sentencing in the juvenile system was 98 days, compared to 246 days for juveniles waived to the adult system.

Research seems more consistent regarding general deterrence; that is, transfer policies seem to do nothing to reduce juvenile crime.[56] Jensen and Metsger examined the deterrent effect of increased adult trials and sentences for juveniles in Idaho. Idaho had mandated in 1981 that youth ages 14 to 18 who were charged with murder, attempted murder, robbery, forcible rape, and aggravated assault be tried in the adult court. They compared Idaho with its two neighborhood states, Montana and Wyoming, in which waiver decisions still required a hearing before the judge. Only in Idaho did juvenile crime increase over the time period.[57] A 1993 *USA Today*/*CNN*/Gallup poll found 73 percent of adults surveyed supported transferring juveniles to adult courts.[58]

Another change in juvenile justice in the 1990s was the introduction of mandatory minimum sentences. Between 1992 and 1995, 15 states plus Washington, DC required a mandatory minimum sentence for certain offenders.[59] Although indeterminate sentences were a hallmark of the early juvenile courts, the idea then was that the youth were released when they had been rehabilitated and were of age. Now, juveniles can be detained in some states until they are 25, and some states have no maximum age at all.[60] By the end of 1997, 42 states allowed the juvenile court to release juvenile's name, address, and/or picture in certain situations. In 30 states, some or all juvenile court proceedings were open to the public, and school officials were allowed to access juvenile court records in some states.[61]

Most state legislation does not specify minimum age limits for juvenile court jurisdiction. As such, courts can develop their own criteria. Maximum ages for original jurisdiction in the juvenile courts range between 15 and 17. Although most states retain control of juveniles only until age 21, California, Montana, Oregon, and Wisconsin allow for juveniles to be held until age 25.[62] Juveniles can be held indefinitely for certain offenses in Colorado, Connecticut, Hawaii, and New Mexico.[63]

As was clear in earlier decades, there are some major problems with housing juveniles and adults in the same facility. Children and youth held in adult detention facilities are eight times more likely to commit suicide, five times more likely to be sexually assaulted, twice as likely to be beaten by staff, and 50 percent more likely to be attacked with a weapon.[64] Additionally, there is always the concern that housing delinquents with more serious offenders creates a school for crime. One Florida juvenile who had been incarcerated with adults had this to say: "I learned how to break into a safe, to get by alarms, other ways to get into houses ... When I get back to the street I won't get caught as easy."[65]

Disproportionate Impact

Another major concern about the juvenile justice system that continued and even escalated in the 1990s is its disproportionate impact on youth of color. Disparity has been found at every phase of the juvenile justice process, but was most significant at the beginning, or arrest, phase.[66] Several studies have affirmed that one of the most important factors officers consider when determining whether to make an arrest is the juvenile's demeanor. Those exhibiting a respectful attitude are less likely to be arrested.[67] "Several factors may explain the differences, but offending rates of minorities is not one of them."[68] In 1999, the Uniform Crime Reports (UCR) listed 2.5 million juvenile arrests. Although white youth at the time comprised 79 percent of the age 10–17 population, they were 72 percent of those arrested. In contrast, blacks were 15 percent of that age group, yet 25 percent of those arrested.[69]

Between 1975 and 1995, the number of juveniles in custody increased 45 percent. The increase for youth of color was even more dramatic. Rates tripled for black youth and quadrupled for Hispanic youth. By 1995, black and Hispanic youth were 28 percent and 17 percent of the population in juvenile facilities, respectively.[70] Black juveniles were 15 percent of the juvenile population, but 26 percent of all youth arrested and 31 percent of youths referred to juvenile court.[71] Studies have found that white youth are more likely to admit guilt, which is viewed favorably by the court system.[72] Additionally, minority youth are less likely to live in two-parent families, which is also viewed favorably by the system as a sign of amenability to treatment.[73] Others have found poor black youths were more likely to be removed from their homes.[74]

Racial disparities are more dramatic in court referrals, where 63 percent of cases involving whites and 76 percent of cases involving black youth were referred to the court. The rate for other races was 77 percent. Disparity is also true in detention—whereas 18 percent of white youth were sent to a detention facility, 25 percent of blacks and 23 percent of other races were. Because of cumulative effects of disparity, nonwhite youths were greatly overrepresented in the number of young people in a correctional facility in 1999. In 1999, minorities were in correctional facilities at rates nearly double their proportion in the population.[75]

Juvenile's Capacity to Understand Court Processes

Another concern that has continued from earlier decades is regarding the ability of juveniles to understand the process and their rights. A 1998 case in Chicago highlighted the dangers of interrogating young people in the same ways that might be used with adults. On August 9, 1998, two African American boys, ages seven and eight, confessed that they killed 11-year-old Ryan Harris because they wanted her bike. Both had been questioned for hours without a parent or guardian present. The boys were released when the lab report found semen on the body matching a convicted adult sex offender.[76]

The case of Lacresha Murray is also illustrative of some of the difficulties with assessing whether juveniles understand what is happening. Murray was 11 years old when she was convicted of criminally negligent homicide in the death of a two-and-a-half-year-old. She was sentenced to 25 years in prison. Her conviction and sentence were based on one piece of evidence: a confession she signed. Lacresha was only 11, and had a learning disability and an IQ of 77. During the four-day interrogation, she was kept away from her family, denied a lawyer, and threatened. She denied she committed the crime 39 times before she caved in. In reality, the victim, Jayla Belton, had suffered tremendous child abuse and had a ruptured liver.[77]

Some maintained that many juvenile homicides are the result of immaturity. Psychologist G. Moffat commented, "We have to teach children not to play in the street so they will not be run over by a vehicle and we have to keep medicines and poison out of reach so they will not eat them. Even though they may know not to play in the street or not to eat poison, until they reach full cognitive development, they cannot fully know *why* they should not do those things and all the possible results of those behaviors."[78] To illustrate, he offered the case of Lionel Tate, 12 years old at the time that he killed 6-year-old Tiffany Eunick while imitating wrestling moves. His attorney's offered this in defense, but were not the only ones making the connection between the World Wrestling Federation (WWF) and major injury/death. In 1999, there were three separate instances in which someone was killed because another was imitating wrestling moves. Although Tate admitted he knew wrestling was not real, it is not likely he understood the full implications of practicing these moves on a six-year-old. Tate was found guilty and sentenced to life in prison without parole.[79]

The Death Penalty for Juveniles

The 1990s saw renewed discussion about using the death penalty with juveniles. Although some called for continued and even expanded use, others were equally vocal in their protest against the practice. California Governor Pete Wilson proposed the death penalty for 14-year-olds. In 1998, Texas legislator Jim Pitts recommended the death penalty for children as young as age 11.[80] By 1998, the United States had executed 143 people for crime they committed as minors.[81] Twenty-two juveniles have been executed in the United States since 1976. Thirteen of those executions occurred in Texas.[82]

On the other hand, a compelling modern argument against executing juveniles has been that of differing brain functioning. Medical research has indicated that the frontal lobes, which control impulse control and reasoning, are the last areas of the brain to develop. These areas of the brain may not fully develop until the early twenties. Therefore, juveniles may not be responsible for their actions to the same degree as adults and, consequently, should not face the most severe sanction.[83]

Another new area of study is the relationship between childhood trauma, such as abuse or neglect, and criminal behavior. A number of studies have indicated that violent victimization significantly increases the risk of future violent behavior. Because juveniles cannot easily escape an abusive environment, death penalty opponents argue it is unfair to execute them for offenses that are a legacy of abuse.[84]

Supreme Court opinions at the start of the twenty-first century set a more lenient tone for juveniles convicted in capital cases. In 2002, the Supreme Court held that it was unconstitutional to execute juveniles who were mentally retarded (*Atkins v. Virginia* (536 U.S. 304, 2002)). The most influential case to date was heard in 2004. In this case, the offender was 17 when he committed a murder in Missouri. He was subsequently convicted and sentenced to death. Simmons appealed on the grounds that the death penalty for offenders under the age of 18 was cruel and unusual. The appeal was launched on the premise of the decision in *Atkins v. Virginia*.[85]

The Missouri Supreme Court agreed with the petitioner and vacated the death sentence. The case then moved to the Supreme Court. The Supreme Court Justices held that executing juveniles violated both the Eighth and Fourteenth Amendments, as both prohibit the execution of offenders who were under the age of 18 at the time of their crime (*Roper v. Simmons* (633 U.S. 1962)). This decision has ended the long-standing debate over the juvenile death penalty and has converted juvenile death sentences to life sentences without parole across the United States. It has also made the United States in line with most of the rest of the world, and all of the developed world.[86]

OTHER LEGISLATION

In the late 1990s, curfews were a popular method to deal with the perceived problem of out-of-control juvenile delinquency. There is a long history of curfews in the United States. In the antebellum South, curfews were used to control slaves as well as free blacks. Additionally, curfews have been used on entire regions during times of emergency, such as during World War II.[87] Juveniles are the most common target for curfew laws. The first juvenile curfew law was enacted in Omaha, Nebraska, in 1880, and by 1900, there were 3,000 juvenile curfew laws across the nation. The number of laws, and enforcement of them, increased during World War II and during the post-war population boom. By 1957, more than 50 percent of cities with a population over 100,000 had a juvenile curfew ordinance. In the mid 1990s, 77 percent of cities with a population of 200,000 or more had juvenile curfew rules. The 1996 Anti-Gang and Youth Violence Act provided $75 million to support curfews and anti-truancy measures.[88] As of 1997, more than 1,000 localities were enforcing juvenile curfew laws.[89]

Proponents of curfews maintain that they reduce juvenile crime, protect juveniles, protect society, and help parents maintain authority. Allegedly, curfew laws epitomize the dual goals of the initial juvenile justice system—to punish yet ensure that the best interest of children are met. Additionally, there is widespread public support for curfew laws, with 92 percent and 77 percent of Cincinnati and Washington, DC residents, respectively, supporting curfew laws in the 1990s.[90]

Opponents maintain juvenile crime is more prominent during the after-school hours—3:00 to 6:00 P.M.—so curfews are not needed. In reality, 80 percent of juvenile offenses occur between 9:00 A.M. and 10:00 P.M.[91] Another argument is that curfews punish juveniles who might have legitimate reasons to be out. Still another argument is that, rather than reinforcing parental authority, they reduce it and put it in the hands of the state. Critics contend curfew laws violate the First and Fourteenth Amendment rights of young people. Further, some are concerned that law enforcement disproportionately enforces curfew laws against poor and minority youth. The Supreme Court has not heard a curfew case, but lower courts have and have generally affirmed them. Most localities have not conducted any empirical assessment to see if curfew laws are effective.[92]

In 1994, Monrovia, California began using a juvenile curfew policy, supposedly because they had a major delinquency problem they needed to address. In reality, all crime was down that year, including acts committed by juveniles. Evaluations demonstrated the policy actually increased noncurfew-related offenses by juveniles during the school months, when the policy was enforced. Arrest rates went back down in the summer months when the policy was not enforced. Curfew violations were disproportionately given to minority youth, and parents of teens who had been arrested were forced to pay $62 per hour in custodial fees.[93] Chicago also saw disparity in enforcement of their curfew laws.[94]

SCHOOL VIOLENCE AND RESPONSES TO IT

The mid-to-late 1990s seemed to be a hotbed of school violence. In reality, schools remained one of the safest places for young people. This is discussed in more detail later. Some have asserted that these incidents received so much attention because they happened in largely white, suburban or rural schools. Historically, violence has occurred in urban schools sporadically, but because it was in poor and often minority-dominated districts, it did not garner the same attention. It was as though it was expected.[95] Although in many ways these incidents are atypical of what happens in schools, several are briefly discussed here because they highlight some of the concerns with juvenile justice explained throughout in the chapter.

February 2, 1996 was the first in a series of student-perpetrated, multiple-victim homicides on school grounds. Many consider the shooting by 14-year-old honor student Barry Loukaitis at Frontier Junior High School to have triggered copycat-type incidents around the country.[96]

On February 2, Loukaitis entered the school in Moses Lake, Washington, dressed as the man with no name from the film *Fistful of Dollars*. He was armed with a high-powered hunting rifle and two pistols. Loukaitis entered his algebra class and took the class hostage. He killed two students, Manual Vela junior and Arnie Fritz, and his algebra teacher, Leona Caires, and seriously wounded several other students. Eventually, physical education teacher Jon Lane overpowered Loukaitis.[97]

Consistent with the trend of the decade, Loukaitis was waived to adult court. Throughout his trial, it became clear that he had a bizarre, if not abusive, home life. He was also bullied at school. This case brought up the concern of copycat media violence. *Rage,* by Stephen King, was one of Loukaitis' favorites and a copy was found in his home. The plot of the book is very similar to what happened at Frontier Junior High School. The protagonist in *Rage* is a high school student who is victimized and bullied and eventually goes insane. Like Loukaitis, he goes to school, holds his class hostage, and kills his teacher as a form of revenge for prior mistreatment.[98]

Loukaitis also seemed to be preoccupied with the film *Natural Born Killers*. Records indicated that he had rented the film numerous times and classmates said he could quote the film's lines by heart. Additionally, Loukaitis was obsessed with Pearl Jam's song *Jeremy,* about a boy who shoots his classmates after repeatedly being taunted by them.[99]

Louakitis plead not guilty by reason of insanity. Defense experts contended that Loukaitis basically lived in a fantasy world, whereas prosecution experts pointed to the planning involved in the incident to conclude Loukaitis was a rational thinker. The jury rejected the insanity plea and Loukaitis was convicted and sentenced to life in prison without parole.[100]

On the morning of October 1, 1997, 16-year-old Luke Woodham beat his mother with a baseball bat and stabbed her to death with a butcher knife while she was sleeping. Three hours later, armed with a rifle that he concealed under his trench coat, Woodham drove to Pearl High School intent on killing Christina Menefee, who had ended their short-lived relationship a year earlier. When he arrived, Woodham entered the school's large indoor courtyard, spotted Menefee and her best friend, Drew, and opened fire. Before the shooting spree ended, seven students were wounded, and both Menefee and Drew were dead. As he attempted to flee the scene, Assistant Principal Joel Myrick apprehended Woodham, who was armed with another pistol he had retrieved from his car during the melee. Less than an hour after the shootings, Woodham was in police custody.[101]

Luke Woodham is serving three life sentences and seven 20-year sentences for the shooting deaths of his mother, Mary Woodham, Christina Menefee, and Lydia Drew, 17, as well as the aggravated assault of seven others. With the exception of his mother, the victims were fellow classmates at Pearl High School in Pearl, Mississippi.[102]

On December 1, 1997, only one month after Luke Woodham's shooting spree at Pearl High School in Mississippi, Michael Carneal opened fire on a prayer group in the lobby of Heath High School in Heath, Kentucky. Carneal, then 14 years old, pleaded guilty but mentally ill to all charges.[103] Like Barry Louakitis, Carneal had suffered merciless torment by his peers. Unlike Loukaitis, he appeared to have the ideal home life, although it was clear he never felt he could measure up to his sister, who was an excellent student, athlete, and was loved in the school and community.[104]

The plea was rejected, and Carneal was sentenced to life in prison for the shooting deaths of three young ladies as well as five counts of attempted murder, and one count of burglary. As noted earlier, the families of the three dead girls brought suit against Carneal as well as 21 media companies, claiming that Carneal's frequent exposure to video games and violent movies contributed to the crimes.[105]

On March 24, 1998, Mitchell Johnson and Andrew Golden, ages 13 and 11, opened fire at students and teachers at the middle school they attended in Jonesboro, Arkansas. The boys had planned the attack and had stockpiled an arsenal of weapons. The attack lasted less than five minutes, but left four students and one teacher dead and another 10 injured. Police captured the two boys trying to exit the woods near the school and make it to their van. There they found over a dozen weapons and a large stock of ammunition.[106]

Unlike most of the other shootings, because of their age, both boys were charged as juveniles and placed into juvenile institutions. On August 12, 2005, amid heavy criticism from the Jonesboro community, Mitchell Johnson was released from a Tennessee facility. His record was wiped clean because he is no longer a juvenile. Johnson does not plan to live in Arkansas. Andrew Golden is scheduled for release in 2007.[107]

On Friday, April 24, 1998, Andrew Jerome Wurst, then 14, used his father's .25 caliber semiautomatic handgun to fatally injure one teacher, John Gillette, and injure another teacher and two students from his school in Edinboro, Pennsylvania. The attack occurred just north of Edinboro at a restaurant where Parker Middle School was hosting an eighth grade dance.[108]

Defense experts maintained Wurst suffered from mental illness. After psychological evaluation, Wurst was determined to be mentally competent and was waived to adult court. One reason offered for Wurst's shooting was that he had recently been rejected by a young lady and had considered suicide as early as age 10. In addition, testimony showed he liked to read Stephen King novels and listen to the music of Marilyn Manson. Instead of going to trial and risking a life sentence without parole, Wurst accepted a plea bargain, in which he plead guilty to third-degree murder. He as sentenced to 30 to 60 years with eligibility for parole in 30 years.[109]

Of course, the most widely known school shooting in the 1990s occurred at Columbine High School in Littleton, Colorado. On April 20, 1999, Eric Harris and Dylan Klebold opened fire on classmates and teachers. Heavily armed, the two killed 12 students and one teacher before killing themselves. After the horrifying incident, which received tremendous amounts of media coverage, many pointed to warning signs as early as 1996. Both boys had written angry and hateful material on the Web, played violent video games, and had been in legal trouble before (they had gone through a diversion program). Pundits, policymakers, educators, and researchers seized the opportunity to examine possible causes and develop interventions. In looking at why the incident occurred, many blamed Harris's and Klebold's parents, the media (in particular, the music of shock-rocker Marilyn Manson), and the leniency they had received from the diversion program. Schools all over responded to the incident with increased hardware and surveillance.[110]

On May 20, 1999, one month to the day after the school shootings at Columbine High School in Littleton, Colorado, Anthony Solomon (known as T.J.) opened fire in the commons area of Heritage High School in Rockdale County, Georgia, a suburb of Atlanta. Although there were no fatalities, six students were wounded, one of them critically. Solomon was sentenced to 60 years, with the possibility of parole after 18 years, after pleading guilty but mentally ill to 29 criminal charges.[111]

Were these incidents really indicative of an epidemic of school violence, as some argued? Evidence suggests otherwise. In reality, school remains one of the safest places for a young person. For instance, although the shootings in Pearl,

West Paducah, Jonesboro, Edinboro, and Springfield left 11 people dead over eight months, this same amount of children are killed by their own parents every two days in the United States.[112] By the end of the 1990s, only 10 percent of school districts across the nation had ever reported an incident of violence.[113]

Although school violence in any form should be considered serious, often the responses to it are far greater than the actual threat. The punitive responses are popular, however, because much of the public has been convinced that young people are all bad—all superpredators waiting to victimize innocent students and teachers. Vincent Schiraldi of the Justice Policy Institute explained, "Today's seniors are no more likely than their parents were to be assaulted, injured, threatened or robbed in high school. Ironically, today's seniors are more likely to be suspended than their parents were."[114]

One of the most popular responses to school violence, whether real or perceived, has been zero tolerance laws. Zero tolerance is a concept taken from the war on drugs. In regard to schools, it emanates from the 1994 Gun-Free Schools Act, which required states to enact mandatory punishments for students found with a firearm on school property.

There are many concerns with zero tolerance. One of these is that few schools have conducted any comprehensive evaluation of whether zero tolerance laws are effective. Another concern is that these laws are applied to silly situations that can be better addressed more informally. For instance, in 1996, 11-year-old Myles Kully shared some juice from his lunch that had been made from home-grown habanero peppers. One of the students burned his eye from the peppers, and Myles was charged with "possession and distribution of a habanero pepper" and suspended for a day.[115]

Yet another concern about zero tolerance laws is that they disproportionately impact specific groups. The *American Journal of Trial Advocacy* found African American males were being suspended and/or expelled at rates 250 times higher than white males.[116] In 1999, Blacks were 16 percent of the enrollment in San Francisco schools but 52 percent of students removed from school for disciplinary reasons.[117]

Still another concern is that zero tolerance laws are simply a pathway to the juvenile justice or adult criminal justice system. Between 2000 and 2004 there was a 71 percent increase in the number of students referred to law enforcement in Denver, Colorado.[118] The American Bar Association has called for the end of zero tolerance policies in schools. In 2001, 400,000 members critiqued zero tolerance, saying it was turning students into criminals.[119]

Zero tolerance was not the only way schools became harsher environments for young people. In the late 1980s and into the 1990s, the Supreme Court upheld a number of forms of school-based searches of students. The searches allowed educators to search students with reasonable suspicion, a more lenient standard than the probable cause required for police-based searches, in *New Jersey v. T.L.O.* in 1985. In 1995 and in 2002, the Supreme Court supported drug testing of students, first of athletes and then of students in extracurricular activities. At the same time that the Supreme Court has broadened the ability of school administrators to search students, state laws have also widened the range of offenses for which administrators must involve police. For instance, in some locations, the law requires that police be involved in searches at school and be alerted if any evidence whatsoever is obtained from a search.[120]

Police also got more involved in school crackdowns. In the summer after the Columbine shooting, several police agencies across the nation taught their SWAT teams how to invade local high schools, and they practiced with mock raids. SWAT teams have also been used in schools to search for drugs.[121]

ALTERNATIVES

Peaceable Schools

Although many schools have followed the get-tough trend, others began to explore more humanistic ways to respond to, and, better yet, prevent school violence. Peaceable classrooms are places where peace-related themes are integrated into the curriculum. They are also classrooms where teachers share power with students, where cooperative efforts are encouraged and supported, where all people are treated with dignity and respect, and where all views are welcomed. Because conflict is inevitable, peaceable classrooms emphasize how to manage conflict in positive and nonviolent ways. Peaceable schools use these same concepts on a broader scale, integrating them into policies and practices for the entire school. Peaceable schools are places where everyone feels important, and where all students have ample opportunity to explore their learning potential. More than simply teaching about peace and justice, peaceable schools recognize that students learn from the way schools are structured and the methods used.[122] To that end, peaceable schools are a comprehensive approach that uses multiple strategies to prevent violence of all sorts and to emphasize social justice for all students.[123]

To date, there has been little research evaluating the effectiveness of the peaceable schools movement. In Tennessee, 75 percent of schools are involved in creating a peaceable environment. From 1997 to 2000, these schools saw a 14 percent drop in suspension rates. This suggests that peaceable schools are working.[124]

The Resolving Conflict Creatively Program (RCCP), widely used in New York, is a similar program that is comprehensive in nature. Evaluations of RCCP have found that students retain more positive behaviors throughout the school year than do students not exposed to the program. Teachers report that students take responsibility for resolving their problem behavior much quicker than they did in the past.[125]

Diversion Programs

In the 1980s and 1990s, many states initiated or expanded diversion programs for youth. Diversion generally refers to "a decision to turn youth away from the official system and handle them via alternative procedures and programs."[126] Drawing from Developmental theories, Labeling theories, and Learning theories, the idea is that juveniles involved in programs outside the formal juvenile justice system will receive the support they need and avoid the labeling and networking with fellow delinquents that occur inside the system. As such, they will be less likely to recidivate.[127] Federal funding in the later 1960s and 1970s spawned a variety of different diversion programs, including job training, alternative schools, and community-service style programs. In particular, the *Gault* case prompted states to find more informal services for delinquent and wayward youth.[128] Since the 1980s and the shift toward more punitive sanctions, diversion has often taken the form of restitution and work programs.[129] Although studies have not necessarily painted an optimistic picture of the successes of diversion, researchers have concluded that it can be very effective if used when offenders are young and when there are many contact hours between the youth and their service provider(s).

Although diversion tends to be popular among those holding more liberal views, even some liberals denounce it. Rather than helping young people, they see it as yet another means of widening the net. Youth who might formerly have evaded any type of involvement in juvenile justice are now processed through a diversion program simply because one exists, critics say.[130] Diversion provides a rationale for shifting discretion from the core of the juvenile court, where it is subject to some types of procedural safeguards, to the periphery of the system, where no procedural safeguards are guaranteed.[131] Girls are overrepresented in diversion programs. Girls are far more likely to have been sent through diversion not for an actual offense, but "for their own good."[132]

State-Level Innovations

At the state level, Massachusetts has been a leader in innovative programming for juveniles, although leaders have often succumbed to pressures to be more traditional. Major criticisms of the Massachusetts juvenile justice system in the 1960s prompted that state to enact some very progressive reforms. Critics claimed the Massachusetts system failed to rehabilitate youth, allowed for their abuse while detained, and released young people who were more dangerous than when they had entered the system. In 1972, under the direction of a bipartisan group of state legislators, Massachusetts abandoned the warehousing of juvenile offenders in reform schools and began utilizing community-based programs. Not only was the new system cheaper, but it seemed effective—by 1985, Massachusetts was 46th out of the 50 states plus Washington, DC in regard to juvenile crime rate.[133] In 1995, however, a crime took place that made the state revert back to their old ways.

On July 23, 42-year-old Janet Downing was stabbed to death in her home in Somerville, Massachusetts, by her neighbor, 15-year-old Eddie O'Brien. After comprehensive evaluations of O'Brien, the judge ruled he should be tried as an adult, making him eligible for release at age 20. That decision was changed on appeal, and O'Brien was tried as an adult, convicted, and sentenced to life without the possibility of parole. Even though O'Brien was given a very serious sentence, there was tremendous outcry about the possibility that he could have served only five years for such a heinous crime. In other states, politicians sited one especially egregious case to advocate more severe sanctions for juvenile offenders.[134]

Another innovative program from Massachusetts was a coordinated community effort targeting at-risk youth. Operation Ceasefire was part of a problem-solving policing effort intended to address escalating violence among juveniles ages 8 to 18. Operation Ceasefire was not innovative because it was more humanistic, per se. Rather, it was innovative because it involved a collaborative effort among many agencies and levels of government. And, unlike many programs, it involved academics and researchers as well as practitioners.[135]

Maryland has also adjusted their approach to juvenile justice, incorporating a more holistic approach. In 1997, Maryland proposed revising their Juvenile Causes Act to reflect the states' use of a balanced and restorative approach. The change was enacted, and Maryland continues to build their juvenile system around the three goals of public safety, offender accountability, and competency and character development.[136] "Maryland's approach to juvenile justice is based on the belief that the juvenile justice system's clients are not just offenders, but victims and communities as well. Therefore, the juvenile justice system is compelled to balance its resources, time and attention among these three clients, holding each accountable to the others."[137] The state has dramatically increased their use of intermediate sanctions as well as the amount and quality of aftercare and educational programs. They have added prevention and intervention efforts to address chronic school truancy and to target at-risk youth. Law enforcement has practiced hot spot policing, based on the knowledge that more than 50 percent of crimes occur in approximately 3 percent of the addresses, which tend to be clustered together.[138]

Community-Based Innovations

Operation Ceasefire was part of a collaborative and comprehensive strategy that was developed between 1994 and 1996 to address Boston's escalating crime rates. Boston experienced an epidemic of youth homicide between the late 1980s and early 1990s. Homicides averaged 44 per year between 1991 and 1995. Operation Ceasefire was implemented in Boston in May 1996 and was directed at gangs. Two other projects, the Boston Gun Project, which aimed at gun suppression and prohibition, and Operation Night Light, a partnership between police and probation, accompanied Operation Ceasefire. Operation Ceasefire focused on illegal gun traffickers and deterring gang violence. The Boston Police Department's Youth Violence Strike Force (YVSF), a multi-agency task force working in collaboration with several agencies and institutions from all levels of government, developed the strategy.[139]

The primary goal of Operation Ceasefire was to warn gangs that violence would no longer be tolerated. Officers targeted non-complying gangs and enforced any outstanding warrants and probation surrenders, which spread the zero tolerance message quickly among the other gangs.[140]

Since Operation Ceasefire, Boston has witnessed a dramatic decrease in homicides. This is most likely due to a combination of the three strategic programs as well as neighborhood policing, tougher youth offender laws, and more prevention and intervention programs. The Boston Police Department won the Innovations in American Government award from the Ford Foundation in 1997, as well as the Herman Goldstein award for best program using problem-solving strategies.[141]

CONCLUSION

In sum, better understanding of the development of offenders helped prompt early intervention, diversion, and more humanistic approaches to juvenile justice. At the same time, the juvenile system continued to become more like the adult system in many ways. One theorist maintained the juvenile justice system has positioned itself to have one of two choices: do everything, or do nothing. That is, because possibilities for leniency for juveniles have been severely limited, courts can either apply the entire, severe sanction, or they can opt to do nothing, believing those sentences too harsh. Barry Feld has argued the juvenile justice system is simply too broken to fix.[142]

Although they agree with Feld that the juvenile court is a mess in a lot of ways, Mark Moore and Stewart Wakeling advocated reconceptualizing the court as a family court system that would emphasize social science research and access to social services.[143] Opponents to abolition maintain it would destroy the good along with the bad.[144] Chapter 7 examines some of these ideas.

NOTES

1. Briscoe, J. (2004). Breaking the cycle of violence: A rational approach to at-risk youth. In S. Holmes & R. Holmes (Eds.). *Violence: A contemporary reader* (pp. 259–277). Upper Saddle River, NJ: Prentice Hall.

2. Benekos, P., & Merlo, A. (2002). Reaffirming juvenile justice. In R. Muraskin, & A. Roberts (Eds). *Visions for change* (3rd ed., pp. 265–286). Upper Saddle River, NJ: Prentice Hall.

3. Snyder, H. & Sickmund, M. (1999). *Juvenile offenders and victims: 1999 National Report.* Washington, DC: Office of Juvenile Justice and Delinquency Prevention.

4. Hyman, I., & Snook, P. (1999). *Dangerous schools.* San Francisco: Jossey-Bass, p. 163.

5. Coontz, S. (2000). *The way we never were: American families and the nostalgia trap.* New York: Basic.

6. Parenti, C. (1999). *Lockdown America.* London: Verso.

7. Ibid.

8. Kappeler, V., Blumberg, M., & Potter, G, (2000). *The mythology of crime and criminal justice.* Prospect Heights, IL: Waveland Press.

9. Goode, E., & Ben-Yehuda, N. (1994). *Moral panics: The social construction of deviance.* Oxford: Blackwell.

10. Males, M. (1999). *Framing youth.* Monroe, ME: Common Courage Press, p. 51.

11. Ibid.

12. Finley, L. (2007). Developmental theories. In L. Finley, *The encyclopedia of juvenile violence* (pp. 63–66). Westport, CT: Greenwood.

13. Loeber, R., Farrington, D., Stouthamer-Loeber, M., Moffit, T., & Caspi, A. (1998). The development of male offending: Key findings from the Pittsburgh youth study. *Studies in Crime and Crime Prevention, 3,* 197–247.

14. Moffitt, T. (1993). "Life-course-persistent" and "adolescent limited" antisocial behavior: A developmental taxonomy. *Psychological Review, 100,* 674–701.

15. Ibid.

16. Katz, J. (1988). *Seductions of crime.* New York: Basic.

17. Gottfredson, M., & Hirschi, T. (1990). *A general theory of crime.* Stanford, CA: Stanford University Press.

18. Ibid.

19. Ibid.

20. Ibid.

21. Hagan, J. (1989). *Structural criminology.* New Brunswick, NJ: Rutgers University Press.

22. Ibid.

23. Ibid.

24. Beaucar, K. (2001, August 8). Spike in female juvenile violence prompts multitude of explanations. *Fox News.* Retrieved May 1, 2006 from www.foxnews.com.

25. Cited in Chesney-Lind, M., & Pasko, L. (2004). *The female offender: Girls, women, and crime* (2nd ed.). Thousand Oaks, CA: Sage, p. 32

26. Finley, L. (2007). Liberation theory. In L. Finley (Ed.). *The encyclopedia of juvenile violence* (pp. 181–183). Westport, CT: Greenwood.

27. Springhall, J. (1998). *Youth, popular culture and moral panics.* New York: St. Martin's Press.

28. Newman, K., Fox, C., Harding, D., Mehta, J., & Roth, W. (2004). *Rampage: The social* roots of school shootings. New York: Basic Books.

29. Bush. B. (2007). Film and juvenile violence. In L. Finley (Ed.). *The encyclopedia of juvenile violence* (pp. 79–80). Westport, CT: Greenwood.

30. Feld, B. (1999). *Bad kids: Race and the transformation of the juvenile court.* New York: Oxford University Press, p. 31.

31. Mintz, S. (2004). *Huck's raft: A history of American childhood.* Cambridge, MA: The Belknap Press of Harvard University Press, p. 338.

32. Brooks, K., Schiraldi, V., & Zeidenberg, J. (1998, July). Schoolhouse hype: Two years later. *Justice Policy Institute/Children's Law Center.* Retrieved January 8, 2001, from www.cjcj.prg/schoolhousehype/shh2.html.

33. Myers, D. (2005). *Boys among men: Trying and sentencing juveniles as adults.* Westport, CT: Greenwood.

34. Ibid.

35. Elikann, P. (1999). *Superpredators: The demonization of our children by the law.* New York: Insight.

36. Salant, J. (2003, March 3). Study finds many teens tried as adults despite inability to understand proceedings. *Rocky Mountain Collegian,* p. 6.

37. Lantigua, J. (2003, February 17). Juveniles doin' the time are learning the crime. *Rocky Mountain News* [online edition]. Retrieved February 19, 2003, from www.rockymountainnews.com.

38. Siegel, L., Welsh, B., & Senna, J. (2003). *Juvenile delinquency: Theory, practice, and law* (8th ed.). Belmont, CA: Wadsworth.

39. Elikann (1999).

40. Myers (2005).

41. Ibid.

42. Ibid.

43. Ibid.

44. Ibid.

45. Ibid.

46. Elikann (1999).

47. Benekos & Merlo (2002).

48. Myers (2005).

49. Lantigua (2003).

50. Myers (2005).

51. Ibid.

52. Benekos & Merlo (2002).

53. Fagan, J. (1995). Separating the men from the boys: The comparative advantage of juvenile versus criminal court sanctions on recidivism among adolescent felony offenders. In J. Howell, B. Krisberg, J. Hawkins, & J. Wilson (Eds.). *A sourcebook: Serious, violent, & chronic juvenile offenders* (pp. 238–260). Thousand Oaks, CA: Sage, p. 254.

54. Elikann (1999).

55. Ibid.

56. Myers (2005).

57. Ibid.

58. Meddis, S. (1993, October 29). Poll: Treat juveniles the same as adult offenders. *USA Today,* pp. A1, A11.

59. Kappeler et al. (2000).

60. Ibid.

61. Torbet, P., & Szymanski, L. (1998). *State legislative responses to violent juvenile crime: 1996–1997 update.* Washington, DC: Office of Juvenile Justice and Delinquency Prevention.

62. Myers (2005).

63. Torbet, P., Gable, R., Hurst, H., Montgomery, I., Szymanski, L., & Thomas, D. (1996). *State responses to serious and juvenile crime* (Report No. NCJ 161565). Washington, DC: Office of Juvenile Justice and Delinquency Prevention.

64. Elikann (1999).

65. Lantigua (2003).

66. Snyder & Sickmund (1999).

67. Lawrence, R. (1998). *School crime and juvenile justice.* New York: Oxford University Press.

68. Benekos & Merlo (2002), p. 68.

69. National Center for Juvenile Justice. (2003). Juvenile arrest rates by offense, sex, and race. *Office of Juvenile Justice and Delinquency Prevention.* Available at http:// ojjdp.ncjrs.org/ojstatbb/excel/JAR_053103.xls.

70. Smith, B. (1998). Children in custody: 20-year trends in juvenile detention, correctional, and shelter facilities. *Crime & Delinquency, 44*(4), 526–543.

71. Poe-Hamagata, E., & Jones, M. (2000). *And justice for some.* San Francisco, CA: National Council on Crime and Delinquency.

72. See Leiber, M. (1994). A comparison of juvenile court outcomes for Native Americans, African Americans, and Whites. *Justice Quarterly, 11,* 257–279. Kempf, Decker, & Bing (1990)

73. See Austin, J. (1995). The overrepresentation of minority youths in the California Juvenile Justice System: Perceptions and realities. In K. Kempf-Leonard, C. Pope, & W. Feyerherm (Eds.). *Minorities in juvenile justice* (pp. 153–178). Thousand

Oaks, CA: Sage; Frazier, C. & Bishop, D. (1995). Reflections on race effects in juvenile justice. In K. Kempf-Leonard, C. Pope, & W. Feyerherm (Eds.). *Minorities in juvenile justice* (pp. 16–46). Thousand Oaks, CA: Sage; Kempf, K., Decker, S., & Bing, R. (1990). *An analysis of apparent disparities in the handling of Black youth within Missouri's juvenile justice systems.* St. Louis: Department of Administration of Justice, University of Missouri-St. Louis; and Krisberg, B. & Austin, J. (1993). *Reinventing juvenile justice.* Newbury Park, CA: Sage.

74. See Leonard, K., & Sontheimer, H. (1995). The role of race in juvenile justice in Pennsylvania. In K. Kempf-Leonard, C. Pope, & W. Feyerherm (Eds.). *Minorities in juvenile justice* (pp. 98–127). Thousand Oaks, CA: Sage; Wu, B. (1997). The effect of race on juvenile justice processing. *Juvenile and Family Court Judges Journal, 48,* 43–51.

75. National Center for Juvenile Justice (2003).

76. Fishman, S. (2002). *The battle for children: World War II, Youth crime, and juvenile justice in twentieth-century France.* Cambridge, MA: Harvard University Press.

77. Elikann (1999).

78. Moffat, G. (2003). *Wounded innocents and fallen innocents.* Westport, CT: Preager, p. 191.

79. Ibid.

80. Males (1999).

81. Fishman (2002).

82. Morreale, M., & English, A. (2004). Abolishing the death penalty, for juvenile offenders: A background paper. *Journal of Adolescent Health, 35,* 335–339.

83. Ibid.

84. Ibid.

85. Oritz, A. (2004). *Cruel and unusual punishment: The juvenile death penalty, evolving standards of decency.* Washington DC: The Juvenile Justice Center of the American Bar Association.

86. Morreale & English (2004).

87. Hemmens, C., & Barrett, K. (1999). Juvenile curfews and the courts: Judicial response to a not-so-new crime control strategy. In T. Calhoun & C. Chapple (Eds.). (2003). *Readings in juvenile delinquency and juvenile justice* (pp. 3–20). Upper Saddle River, NJ: Prentice Hall.

88. Ibid.

89. Ibid.

90. Crowell, A. (1996, August). Minor restrictions: The challenge of juvenile curfews. *Public Management,* 4–12.

91. Males (1999).

92. Hemmens & Barret (1999).

93. Males (1999).

94. Dohrn, B. (2001). "Look out kid, it's something you did" zero tolerance for children. In W. Ayers, B. Dohrn, & R. Ayers (Eds.). *Zero tolerance* (pp. 89–113). New York: The New Press.

95. DiGiuilio, R. (2001). *Educate, medicate, or litigate? What teachers, parents and administrators must do about student behavior.* New York: Corwin.

96. Fox, J., Elliot, D., Kerlikowske, R., Newman, S., & Christenson, W. (2003). Bullying prevention is crime prevention. Washington, DC: Fight Crime: Invest in Kids. http://www.fightcrime.org/reports/BullyingReport.pdf 2003.

97. Ibid.

98. Ibid.

99. Ibid.

100. Ibid.

101. Popyk, L. (1998, November 9). Luke's tormented world. *Cincinnati Post,* 1.

102. Ibid.

103. Ibid.

104. Newman et al. (2004)

105. Ibid.

106. Ruddell, R., & Mays, L. (2003). Examining the arsenal of juvenile gunslingers: Trends and policy implications. *Crime and Delinquency,* 49, 231–252.

107. Ibid.

108. DeJong, W., Epstein, J., & Hart, T. (2003). Bad Things Happen in Good Communities: The Rampage Shooting in Edinboro, Pennsylvania, and Its Aftermath. In Mark H. Moore, Carol V. Petrie, Anthony Braga, and Brenda L. McLaughlin (Eds.). *Deadly Lessons: Understanding Lethal School Violence* (pp. 70–100). Washington, DC: The National Academies Press.

109. Ibid.

110. Ruddell & Mays (2003).

111. Newman et al. (2004).

112. Males (1999).

113. Kappeler et al. (2000).

114. Cited in Jones, L. (2001). Students report school crime at same level as 1970s but the use of suspension doubles. *Justice Policy Institute.* Retrieved October 2, 2001 from: www.cjcj.org/sss/.

115. Hyman & Snook (1999)

116. Polakow-Suransky, S. (1999). *Access denied.* Ann Arbor, MI: Student Advocacy Center.

117. Akom, A. (2001). Racial profiling at school: The politics of race and discipline at Berkeley High. In W. Ayers, B. Dohrn, & R. Ayers (Eds.). *Zero tolerance* (pp. 51–63). New York: The New Press.

118. Ibid.

119. ABA recommends ending "zero tolerance" policies in school. (2001, February 21). *Jefferson City News Tribune* [online edition]. Available at www.newstribune.com/stories/022101/wor_0221010033.asp.

120. Beger, R. (2002). Expansion of police power in public schools and the vanishing rights of students. *Social Justice, 29*(1–2), pp. 119–130.

121. Finley, L. & Finley, P. (2005). *Piss off!* Monroe, ME: Common Courage.

122. Eisler, R. (2000). *Tomorrow's children.* Boulder, CO: Westview.

123. Caulfield, S. (2000, January). Creating peaceable schools. *Annals, AAPSS, 567,* 170–185.

124. Ibid.

125. Deutsch, M. (1993). Educating for a peaceful world. *American Psychologist,* *48*(2), 510–517.

126. Ezell, M. (1992). Juvenile diversion: The ongoing search for alternatives. In I. Schwartz (Ed.). *Juvenile justice and public policy* (pp. 45–58). New York: Lexington Books, pp. 45–46.

127. Ibid.

128. Feld (1993). Criminalizing the American juvenile court. In M. Tonry (Ed.). *Crime and justice: A Review of research* (pp. 197–280). Chicago: The University of Chicago Press.

129. Ezell (1992).

130. Ibid.

131. Feld (1993).

132. Feinman, C. (1985). Criminal codes, criminal justice, and female offenders: New Jersey as a case study. In I. Moyer (Ed.). *The changing roles of women in the criminal justice system.* Prospect Heights, IL: Waveland Press.

133. Elikann (1999).

134. Ibid.

135. Finley (2007).

136. Simms, S. (1997). Restorative juvenile justice: Maryland's legislature affirms commitment to juvenile justice reform. *Corrections Today, 57,* 94–98.

137. Ibid., p. 94.

138. Ibid.

139. Kennedy, D. (1997, March). Juvenile gun violence and gun markets in Boston. *National Institute of Justice.* Available at: www.ncjrs.gov/pdffiles/fs000160.pdf

140. Kennedy, D., Braga, A., & Peihl, A. (2004). *Reducing gun violence: The Boston* gun project's Operation Ceasefire. New York: Diane Publishing Co.

141. Operation Ceasefire. (n.d.). Program in Criminal Justice Policy and Management. Available from: http://www.ksg.harvard.edu/criminaljustice/research/bgp.htm

142. Feld (1999).

143. Moore, M., & Wakeling, S. (1997). Juvenile justice: Shoring up the foundations. In M. Tonry (Ed.). *Crime and justice: A review of research* (pp. 253–301). Chicago: The University of Chicago Press.

144. Orlando, F. & Crippen, G. (1994). The rights of children and the juvenile court. In I. Schwartz (Ed.). *Juvenile justice and public policy: Toward a national agenda* (pp. 89–100). New York: Lexington.

7

Post 2000 and Suggestions for the Future

In reviewing the trends in juvenile justice to date, it appears that the United States is at a crossroads. On one hand, punitive trends have continued and even expanded. The concern about crime and violence became even more salient after the terrorist attacks of September 11, 2001. Polls repeatedly showed Americans to be more fearful, and many supported almost any intervention they were told would protect the country.[1] Often, these interventions were simply lip service, and some may even make us less safe. Certainly some interventions threaten important civil liberties.

The juvenile courts today are also a mixture of good and bad, helpful and harmful, protective and punitive. Educator Bill Ayers commented,

The modern Juvenile Court embodies the broken legacy of child-saving, which is to day it is of two minds; one of its goals, to rescue the innocent young from their depraved parents and the sewers of their circumstances; the other, to rectify the behavior of bad children through a regimen of strict discipline, inflexible rules and routines, and unsparing punishment. Juvenile Court is a two-headed monster created for both assignments, and fitted for neither.[2]

Attitudes about young people continue to vacillate as well. Again, Ayers highlighted the views of youth:

Young people in Juvenile Court are simultaneously pure *and* rotten, immaculate *and* corrupt, angels *and* brutes. We must love and understand the little unformed souls, even as we beat the devil out of the wicked, wayward youth. These seemingly contradictory ideas are united by a single, severe assumption: *We*—the respectable, the prosperous, the superior, and (especially in modern times) the professional— know what is best for *Them*—the masses, the poor, the outcast, the wretched of the earth—in short, our clients. We know what is best for them at all times and in all circumstances and without a doubt. Of course, this stance leads to a kind of self- justifying, insistent piousness, which in turn leads to disaster after disaster in both policy and practice. Other people are made into the objects of our interest and experi- mentation. They are rendered voiceless and faceless.[3]

On the other hand, there are many examples of alternative programs in juvenile justice, schools, and communities that show great promise. Three in particular will be addressed in this chapter—Therapeutic Jurisprudence, Restorative Justice, and specialized courts.

CONTINUED CONCERNS

Abuse in Detention

Abuse of young people in detention continues to be a major concern. This is true in traditional juvenile and adult detention facilities as well as in other detention settings. In the fall of 2000, several lawsuits against the state of Louisiana, charging that young inmates were being denied food, necessities, and medical care, were settled. Additionally, staff members were charged with regularly beating inmates. The facility in question was a private prison in Jena, run by Wackenhut Corrections Corporation.[4] Some of the most egre- gious forms of abuse took place at the Tallulah Correctional Center for Youth in Louisiana. The facility was opened in 1994 and run by the private com- pany Trans America.[5] The case of Paul Choy is illustrative of the worst kind of abuse. Choy was killed in 1992 when guards used a dangerous restraint. The autopsy also revealed evidence Choy had been anally raped.[6] The Pahokee Youth Development Center in northern Florida has also been described as an abusive environment. Opened in 1997 by the private company Correctional Services Corporation (CSC), it was supposed to help save taxpayers money while reducing juvenile crime. In reality, the facility was cutting costs on education and other programming for young people, and allegations of abuse were rampant.[7] In October 2006, the *Miami Herald* reported concerns about abuse of juveniles at the Greenville Hills Academy in Florida. Youth detained in the facility claim to have been choked by guards using harmful restraints, and at least one likely suffered a broken collarbone in early October 2006. The facility has been the subject of 30 abuse allegations in the previous two years.[8] A trainer at a juvenile facility explained on the Web site nospank.net the mentality many have: "If I can't make a kid puke or piss his pants on his first day, I'm not doing my job."

Because females are more likely to have experienced abuse in the past, research has concluded that they are more likely to enter the juvenile justice system suffering from depression or Post Traumatic Stress Disorder (PTSD).[9] One study found 92 percent of girls in the California juvenile justice system had been victims of psychological, sexual, or physical abuse.[10] Unfortunately, there are still few programs available that specifically address the unique needs of males and females. Because females only constitute 13 percent of juveniles in detention or correction programs, they are often excluded from large-scale studies and not considered when programs are developed.[11] A study by the San Francisco chapter of the National Organization for Women found that in 1993 that only 8.7 percent of the city's programming was specific to the needs of girls.[12]

Juveniles' Understanding of Court Processes

Research in the new millennium continues to question whether young people can understand the legal process and are capable of waiving their rights. In 2003, the MacArthur Foundation released a study saying that children under the age of 16 could not necessarily understand legal proceedings. In fact, their understanding was no better than that of adults who had been judged incompetent by the courts.[13]

Juvenile Offenders and Mental Illness

As the number of young people suffering from mental illness grows, so do concerns about their involvement in the juvenile justice system. Approximately 20 percent of juvenile offenders are suffering from a severe mental disorder. Thirty percent have been diagnosed with attention deficit hyperactivity disorder (ADHD) and mood disorders (bipolar, manic depressive), respectively. Females are more likely to suffer from anxiety disorders and are six times more likely to have posttraumatic stress disorder (PTSD) than are males.[14] Another study found that 74 percent of females and 66 percent of females met the criteria for a mental disorder. Almost half of the females in their study were found to have a substance abuse disorder.[15]

The rates are even greater for violent juvenile offenders; some 90 percent have a mental disorder of some sort and approximately 70 percent have demonstrated psychotic symptoms.[16] Effective January 2003, H.R. 2198 requires a mental health screening for all youth entering the juvenile justice system.[17] One study concluded that juveniles with mental or emotional disorders stayed in detention 36 percent longer than did all other detainees.[18]

Public Juvenile Records

The 1994 Jacob Wetterling Act requires that sex offenders register when they have committed a sex crime against a minor or a violent sex crime.[19] As laws mandating that sex offenders register online in offender databases have grown in popularity, some have expressed concern that they contradict an important goal of juvenile justice: keeping juvenile records closed to the public. Proponents of the laws suggest that the public has the right to know about sex offenders, who many believe are "never reformed" and will inevitably offend again. Others maintain that the list of offenses requiring registration is too broad. Some states require individuals convicted of statutory rape to register. Thus offenders are labeled and negatively stigmatized for incidents that carry little threat to the general public. A federal bill under consideration in 2006 would require states to put juveniles on public registries, even when their cases are heard in juvenile court.[20] Leah DuBac, age 10 at the time, and her 8- and 5-year-old brothers "flashed" each other and play-acted sex while clothed. At age 12, DuBac pleaded guilty to criminal sexual conduct charges, which required her to register as a sex offender and remain on the registry until age 37. DuBac believes she has received hate mail and has been turned down for jobs and internships as a result of the registry. Mark Chaffin, research director at the National Center on Sexual Behavior of Youth at the University of Oklahoma said juvenile sex offenders are far less likely to reoffend than are adult sex offenders, citing rates between 5 and 15 percent for juveniles and 20 to 25 percent for adults.[21]

In response to these concerns, some states changed their laws in 2006. Vermont no longer requires statutory rape offenders to register, called a "Romeo and Juliet" exception. Missouri does not put juveniles on its public registry at all, and allows teens guilty of statutory rape to be removed from the non-public version of the registry.[22] Chaffin argued that, "The whole logic of a juvenile justice system is that your behavior at 8, 9, 10 or even 13 or 14 should not stigmatize you for life."[23]

Juvenile Boot Camps

One particular type of intervention that gained popularity in the 1990s has been both applauded and denounced in the twenty-first century. Boot camps are a form of alternative sanction intended to be less severe than incarceration but more severe than punishment. Generally based on a military basic training model, boot camps for male and female adult as well as youth offenders exist throughout the country. In 2000, there were 56 boot camps for juveniles in 26 states.[24] The roots of correctional boot camps lie in the 1888 Elmira Reformatory in New York. In 1888, the use of inmate labor became illegal (following the Yates law), so prison administrators had to find alternative ways to occupy inmates' time. Administrator Zebulon Brockway came up with the idea of using military-style training. Few programs followed Brockway's lead, however, perhaps due to the rehabilitation focus of the era. They gelled nicely with the "get tough" climate in the 1980s, however, and were "reborn" in Georgia and Oklahoma in 1983. The climate in the 1980s emphasized individual responsibility and boot camps were viewed as a way to hold offenders accountable. In fact, some boot camps were called accountability programs. Additionally, boot camps received a great deal of media coverage. They make for a strong visual image of "offenders paying for their crimes" by being yelled at by drill sergeants.[25] Because people are familiar with the idea of military basic training—either by having been through, knowing someone who has, or having seen depicted in the media—these programs had face validity.[26] Because the boot camp model includes both punitive and rehabilitative components (at least theoretically), it has received support from people on either side of the political spectrum.[27] By the start of 1990, there were more than 21 programs for adults in 14 states, with most considering programs for juveniles.[28]

Typically, offenders spend 90–120 days in the boot camp in lieu of a traditional prison sentence. In some cases, boot camps are used in conjunction with a shorter prison sentence. Generally, boot camps include a variety of quasi-military features. This might involve military dress, titles, drills, and ceremonies. The atmosphere also follows the military basic training model in that the participants, called cadets, work together and, if they complete the entire program, graduate together. Most people admitted to boot camps are young people who have committed nonviolent offenses and who have not previously been incarcerated.[29] In one analysis of 38 boot camps for juveniles, 40 percent of the programs were found to accept violent offenders.[30]

Proponents maintain boot camps help inmates reform their behavior, learn obedience and organization, and are a cost-efficient way to reduce overcrowding. Research with offenders serving time in boot camps found they perceive the camp to be more punitive than traditional or other alternative forms of punishment.[31] Because there are a number of forms of boot camps, it is difficult to evaluate their effectiveness as a whole. Indeed, different programs have different goals. Studies assessing the goals of juvenile boot camps have found punishment to be fairly low on the list, with the most important goals being safety, academic education, and rehabilitation.[32] Other research has found reducing prison overcrowding to be a primary goal. An evaluation of eight boot camps for adults found participants to be more positive about their experience than those in traditional prisons.[33] Another study found that juveniles in boot camps were less antisocial, less impulsive, and less prone to risk-taking upon completion of the program, in contrast to inmates in traditional programs, who were significantly more antisocial, more impulsive, and took more risks after completion.[34]

Critics maintain boot cams, because of their confrontational nature, cannot truly emphasize treatment. They fail to offer the supportive environment needed for long-term attitudinal and behavioral change.[35] Others maintain that they are prone to abuse of inmates,[36] are not individualized, and perpetuate an "us versus them" mentality that can be dangerous.[37] Further, critics maintain that they teach people to accept authority without question.[38] Self-reports comparing fear of physical danger between those incarcerated in traditional facilities and those in boot camps have found no significant difference in reported fear.[39] Critics also maintain that boot camps do not reduce recidivism any better than other programs. Research has supported this contention.[40] Additionally, boot camps have not been found to increase involvement in work or school programs[41] and they suffer from high dropout rates—in some states as high as 50 percent.[42]

Another concern is whether boot camps can meet the needs of both females and males. Some maintain that, because they are designed for males and have been largely used with male offenders, the programs will not help rehabilitate female offenders. Further, there is concern that females will face sexual harassment or other forms of discrimination in a male-dominated environment. One study found women in boot camps felt more positive about the experience than did males.[43] Like male offenders, female offenders who completed the boot camp program were less antisocial and held more positive attitudes, according to another study.[44] An analysis of females' treatment in boot camps found females reported more problems with sexual harassment and verbal abuse than did male offenders.[45]

In November 2006, charges of aggravated manslaughter were filed against seven former guards and one nurse at a boot camp in Panama City, Florida, for the March 2006 death of 14-year-old Martin Lee Anderson.[46] Evidence of abuse as well as inadequate supervision and negligent medical attention have gained Florida media attention since the incident. In general, there has been an increase in the number of private boot camp or behavior modification facilities. Author M. Szalavitz maintained that, since the later 1970s, all someone had to do was yell "drugs" and many parents would support horrible things being done to "fix" their child. Many young people who were sent to private "treatment" facilities never used drugs at all.[47]

SCHOOL ISSUES

Zero tolerance laws continue to be popular with the public and with conservative politicians. As noted in Chapter 6, proponents of zero tolerance laws continue to argue that they eliminate the chance for discrimination, as they authorize blanket treatment of all juveniles committing specified offenses. The swift, certain message that unwanted behavior will not be accepted is allegedly a deterrent for offenders.

Yet the equality argument obviously falls short, as disparities in the application of zero tolerance laws continue to be clear. A study of schools in Denver, Colorado, revealed black and Latino students were 70 percent more likely to be suspended that their white peers, despite no evidence that their behavior is worse.[48] Further, opponents maintain there is no credible evidence that zero tolerance laws are effective in reducing unwanted behaviors. Additionally, because some administrators assume they have no flexibility in regard to applying the laws, there have been many misapplications. For instance, an Oregon high school forbid a student from displaying a photo of her brother and other Marines because the guns in the photo violated the school's zero tolerance law.[49] A 14-year-old was suspended for a year when drug dogs indicated she had prohibited substances in her locker. The problem turned out to be prescription hormones she takes for polycystic ovarian disease, which she had forgotten to check in at the office.[50] A 10-year-old in Pennsylvania was handcuffed and hauled out of the school by police when she brought a pair of scissors to school to use on a school project.[51] In any of these cases, administrators should consider the totality of the circumstances.

Another continued concern is that zero tolerance laws simply widen the net into the juvenile justice system. In 2005, Advancement Project, a racial justice organization, released a study showing zero tolerance policies have pushed young people into the juvenile justice system. Many times, these students have committed nonviolent offenses—for instance, in Palm Beach County, Florida, a 14-year-old girl was charged with battery for pouring milk on the head of a classmate.[52] Certainly zero tolerance policies are widely used in many areas. A study of Denver, Colorado, public schools between 2000 and 2004 found a 71 percent increase in the number of students referred to police.[53] Some researchers have maintained the "school-to-prison pipeline" in New Orleans was exacerbated by Hurricane Katrina. Prior to Hurricane Katrina, suspension and expulsion were popular with educators in New

Orleans. In 2003–2004, two high schools in Orleans Parish suspended over 40 percent of their students. After the hurricane, high schools have continued to use suspension and expulsion at incredible rates. At one high school, 52 students were suspended in one day for tardiness. One student was arrested for trespassing when he came to school to get his homework despite having been suspended.[54]

Zero tolerance laws have been enforced with students of all ages. In 2005, a Yale University study found preschoolers in Pennsylvania were three times more likely to be expelled from school than older students, although the state expelled fewer students than did many others. The highest rates were in New Mexico, where 21.1 percent of preschool students (students not yet in kindergarten) were expelled. The study found students were most likely to be expelled for ongoing behavioral problems, rather than just one incident. Some have been expelled for zero tolerance violations, including bringing a water pistol to school.[55]

PROMISING ALTERNATIVES?

Alternatives to Traditional Juvenile Justice

"Crime—fear—withdrawal—isolation—weakened community bonds—more crime. All of us, victims, offenders, and community members, are caught in a downward spiral where more crime leads to greater fear and increased isolation and distrust among community members, leading to even more crime."[56] These comments point to the need for more community-centered forms of justice. As it is, crime control efforts have rarely focused on victims. Nor have they really addressed the impact of crime and delinquency on the community. Despite the claims made by progressives (documented in the early chapters of this book), neither victims nor the community have been adequately considered in juvenile justice. Gordon Bazemore wrote,

The effects of this process are magnified with youth. During adolescence the need to belong, have a place that is valued, and be bonded to others intensifies. Youth who are not bonded to conventional community institutions such as school, work, religious and recreational organizations are much more likely to engage in criminal behavior. At the time youth most need to be connected, conventional adults are likely to pull away from them because of extreme styles of dress, music, language, etc. Media stories about youth crime promote a generalized fear of young people among adults. That fear is both deeply disturbing but at the same time provides a sense of power to adolescents and create image problems for even those who are not engaged in criminal behavior.[57]

Restorative justice, often called RJ, aims to correct the inadequacies of both punitive and treatment-based approaches to juvenile justice. "Both punitive and treatment approaches place the offender in a passive role as the object of services on the one hand, and punishment and surveillance on the other. Casting offenders in such roles requires no positive, constructive actions on their part."[58]

Restorative justice sees crime as an act against both a person and the broader community, in contrast to the retributive position that crime is an offense against the state. Restorative justice is a community-focused approach to crime that places the victim, not the state, at the center. It is intended to hold offenders accountable by requiring them to repay the harm caused by their offense. Unlike traditional criminal justice, a characteristic of RJ is its creativity. That is, victims are allowed to voice their ideas about what would help repair the harm. Likewise, community representatives typically voice their ideas as well. Because crime emanates from the community and impacts the community, the community must be involved in the process.[59] Although not new, RJ programs emerged in the United States in the 1970s with an experimental program in the Minnesota Department of Corrections. By the late 1990s, there were approximately 300 RJ programs across the country.[60]

The following are the primary goals for balanced and restorative juvenile justice: accountability, competency, and public safety. Juveniles are to take responsibility for their actions. In contrast to traditional juvenile justice, this is not accountability to the state to complete a specific number of type of program or a designated stay in a detention center. Rather, accountability is to the victim(s).[61] Competency "is not the mere absence of bad behavior."[62] Instead, competent juveniles have obtained educational, vocational, social, and civic awareness in order to become productive adults. Because locking offenders up does not entirely ensure public safety, balanced and restorative justice seeks to strengthen the community's capacity to be safe by empowering citizens to get involved.

Evaluations of RJ programs tend to find them well received, and many find decreased recidivism rates when compared to similar youth who are processed through the juvenile justice system. One study found a significant difference in re-offense rates by violent juvenile offenders, although they found no significant difference among property offenders.[63] Another study found 80 percent of victims to be satisfied with the restorative justice process and reduced offending among non-violent, first-time juvenile offenders.[64]

As noted in previous chapters, many so-called rehabilitative or therapeutic programs simply serve to widen the net. RJ programs emerged from this concern, although interestingly critics have contended they now also widen the net. Some fear that RJ programs result in sanctions against youth who previously would have been left out of the system completely.[65] Some RJ programs widen the net of social control because they are not used as alternatives to incarceration. Rather, offenders who would not have otherwise been processed by the formal system, are required to pay restitution or complete some form of community service. If they fail to do so, they are incarcerated.[66]

Alternative Approaches Within the Juvenile Justice System

An alternative philosophy is Therapeutic Jurisprudence. "The fundamental principle underlying therapeutic jurisprudence is the selection of a therapeutic option—an option that promotes health and does not conflict with other normative values of the legal system."[67] The idea is that the individual, not just the facts of the case, is critical, and attending to his or her needs provides for a more effective resolution.[68] This seems like a natural fit with juvenile justice, at least based on its historical foundations. Therapeutic jurisprudence is not paternalistic or coercive. Rather, it suggests we factor into our thinking about justice concerns about the impact of law on emotional life and psychological well-being.[69] An analysis of drug court programs with juveniles found that these programs offer a more therapeutic, and consequently, more effective, means of addressing juvenile drug offenders.[70]

Alternative Dispute Resolution (ADR) programs have been integrated into many juvenile courts. There are three types of ADR: mediation, in which all involved parties accept a nonbonding solution; family group conferencing, which involves the entire family in discussing the problem and solutions to it; and peer courts, where youth act as juries and in other court-related roles for their peers. ADR helps alleviate the lack of resources most states have to address juvenile crime. Because it is outside the formal institution of juvenile justice, ADR allows for more creative problem solving. Additionally, since the juvenile and his/her family is involved in the process, it can be a source of empowerment. Like restorative justice, research seems to indicate that offenders are more likely to honor agreements that they have had a role in creating.[71]

Another strategy that has been helpful in dealing with youth crime is the creation of unified family courts. The American Bar Association describes unified family courts this way: "A unified family court combines all the essential elements of traditional family and juvenile courts into one entity and contains other resources, such as social services, critical to the resolution of a family's problems. It is a comprehensive court with jurisdiction over all family-related legal matters. The structure of a unified family court promotes the resolution of family disputes in a fair, comprehensive, and expeditious way. It allows the court to address the family and its long-term needs as well as the problems of the individual litigant."[72] These courts eliminate many of the jurisdictional barriers between courts and can streamline the access for a family to needed services.[73]

Some have recommended adding a number of specialty courts for juveniles. These courts are positioned to reach the unique needs of specific types of offenders. Teen courts, drug courts, and gun courts are three types of specialized courts that have demonstrated some success. Teen courts, alternately called youth courts or peer courts, emerged in the early 1990s. By 1998, there were more than 450 teen court programs across the country.[74] Although there are several different models of teen courts, the most commonly used is an adult judge with youth attorneys, jurors, clerks, and court personnel.[75]

Drug courts are more common in the adult criminal justice system. Generally, drug courts require offenders to undergo treatment, to receive strict monitoring, and to submit to regularly urinalysis.[76] One study found juvenile drug court participants were less likely to recidivate than juveniles assigned standard probation. The majority of participants in their study of Maricopa County, Florida, however, did not meet program requirements and ended up on probation or in a detention facility.[77]

Gun courts generally target first-time nonviolent offenders. Many require coursework on weapons, as well as presentation by experts and victims about the impact of gun violence.[78] Although all the specialized courts are positive in addressing the variations in types of offending and the ability to connect youth to specific forms of social service, a drawback is that they typically require offenders to state their guilt.

CONCLUSIONS

In many ways, the United States has been a global leader in the treatment of youth. The development of juvenile courts spread to other countries as, globally, many recognized the differences between juveniles and adults and the need to treat them differently. On the other hand, the United States has lagged behind. To date, the United States has not ratified the United Nations Convention on the Rights of the Child, which affirms that youth are vulnerable and in need of special attention. Until the twenty-first century, the United States still allowed the execution of juveniles. Because crime became a major political campaign issue in the later 1960s, the general push politically has been toward more punitive sanctions and approaches to juvenile justice. Yet, despite the widespread belief that lenient systems increase crime, international comparisons tend to show otherwise. Decriminalizing petty offenses for people under the age of 15 in Austria, for instance, had no significant impact on juvenile crime rates.[79]

As this book has documented, both fear *of* and fear *for* young people result in systems and policies that send mixed messages to young people. Systems and interventions that either patronize or punish young people are also not generally effective. As we move farther into the twenty-first century, it is imperative that we consider our beliefs about young people in order to create policies and programs that will be more useful in preventing and responding to youth delinquency. Dialogue about these beliefs and their implications should occur among and between people in various institutions dealing with youth, including but not limited to educators, lawyers, judges, police, and social workers. Parents also should be involved in discussions about youth development and understanding. Do we believe that youth are indeed developmentally different than adults? If so, how does that translate into educational programming? What legislation is appropriate? How should police interact with young people? Should juveniles be given more or less constitutional guarantees? Or, would it be best to overhaul both juvenile and adult justice, operating from a more victim-centered, restorative approach? Only with more dialogue will we be able to create systems and policies that are proactive, rather than fear based.

NOTES

1. Chermak, S. (2003). Marketing fear: Representing terrorism after September 11th. *Journal for Crime, Conflict, and the Media, 1*(1), 5–22.

2. Ayers, W. (1997). *A kind and just parent: The children of juvenile court.* Boston: Beacon Press, p. 41

3. Ibid., p. 41.

4. Butterfield, F. (2000, September 8). Settling suit, Louisiana abandons private youth prisons. *New York Times,* A14.

5. Gaes, G. (2002). Managing the juvenile offender population through classification and programming. In G. Katzman (Ed.). *Securing our children's future* (pp. 147–174). Washington, DC: The Brookings Institute.

6. Riok, J. (2006, April). Deadly restraint. *Nospank.net.* Retrieved February 11, 2007 from www.nospank.net/camps.

7. Press, E., & Washburn, J. (2002). Privatization within the juvenile justice system must be stopped. In A. Nakaya (Ed.). (2005). *Juvenile crime: Opposing viewpoints* (pp. 187–192). Farmington Hills, MI: Greenhaven.

8. Miller, C., & Caputo, M. (2006, October 14). New claims of abuse at boys camp. *The Miami Herald,* pp. 1–2A.

9. Chesney-Lind, M. (2001). The juvenile justice system must address the needs of girls. In A. Nakaya (Ed.). (2005). *Juvenile crime: Opposing viewpoints* (pp. 178–186). Farmington Hills, MI: Greenhaven.

10. Acoca, L., & Dedel, K. (1998). *No place to hide: Understanding and meeting the needs of girls in the California Juvenile Justice System.* San Francisco, CA: National Council on Crime and Delinquency.

11. Quinn, M., Poirier, J., & Garfinkel, L. (2005). Girls with mental health needs in the juvenile justice system: Challenges and inequities confronting a vulnerable population. *Exceptionality, 13*(2), pp. 125–139.

12. Chesney-Lind, M., & Pasko, L. (2004). *The female offender: Girls, women, and crime.* Thousand Oaks, CA: Sage.

13. Salant, J. (2003, March 3). Study finds many teens tried as adults despite inability to understand proceedings. *Rocky Mountain Collegian,* p. 6.

14. Lyons, J. (2001). Mental health service needs of juvenile offenders: A comparison of detention, incarceration, and treatment settings. *Children's Services, 4,* 69–86.

15. Ibid.

16. Ibid.

17. Teplin, L., Abram, K., McClelland, G., Dulcan, M., & Mericle, A. (2002). Psychiatric disorders in youth in juvenile detention. *Archives of General Psychiatry, 59*(12), 1133–1143.

18. Seltzer, T. (2004). Mentally ill youth should not be placed in the juvenile justice system. In A. Nakaya (Ed.). (2005). *Juvenile crime: Opposing viewpoints* (pp. 168–177). Farmington Hills, MI: Greenhaven.

19. Scholle, A. (2000, July). Sex offender registration. *FBI Law Enforcement Bulletin, 69,* p. 17

20. Moore, M. (2006, July 10). Sex crimes break the lock on juvenile records. *USA Today* [online edition].

21. Ibid.

22. Ibid.

23. Ibid., p. 2.

24. Armstrong, G. (2004). Boot camps as a correctional option. In D. MacKenzie & G. Armstrong (Eds.). *Correctional boot camps: Military basic training or a model for corrections?* (pp. 7–15). Thousand Oaks, CA: Sage.

25. Ibid.

26. Gauthier, A., & Reichel, P. (1989). *Boot camp corrections: A public reaction.* Paper presented at the annual meeting of the Academy of Criminal Justice Sciences, Washington, DC.

27. Armstrong (2004).

28. MacKenzie, D. (1990). Boot camp prisons: Components, evaluations, and empirical issues. *Federal Probation, 54*(3), 44–52.

29. MacKenzie, D., & Parent, D. (2004). Boot camp prisons for young offenders. In D. MacKenzie & G. Armstrong (Eds.). *Correctional boot camps: Military basic training or a model for corrections?* (pp. 16–25). Thousand Oaks, CA: Sage.

30. MacKenzie, D., & Rosay, A. (2004). Correctional boot camps for juveniles. In D. MacKenzie & G. Armstrong (Eds.). *Correctional boot camps: Military basic training or a model for corrections?* (pp. 26–45). Thousand Oaks, CA: Sage.

31. Wood, P., & Grasmick, H. (1999). Toward the development of punishment equivalencies: Male and female inmates rate the severity of alternative sanctions compared to prison. *Justice Quarterly, 16*(1), 19–50.

32. MacKenzie, D., & Souryal, C. (1994). *Multi-site evaluation of shock incarceration: Executive summary.* Report to the National Institute of Justice. Washington, DC: National Institute of Justice.

33. Ibid.

34. MacKenzie, D., Styve, G., & Gover, A. (1998). Performance based standards for juvenile corrections. *Corrections Management Quarterly, 2,* 28–35.

35. Armstrong (2004).

36. Morash, M., & Rucker, L. (1990). A critical look at the idea of boot camp as a correctional reform. *Crime and Delinquency, 36,* 204–222.

37. Armstrong (2004).

38. MacKenzie & Parent (2004).

39. McKenzie, Styve, & Gover (1998).

40. See Bottcher, J., Isorena, T., & Belnas, M. (1996). LEAD: A boot camp and intensive parole program: An impact evaluation, second year findings. Ion, CA: Department of the Youth Authority, Research Division; MacKenzie (1997).

41. Mackenzie, D., & Brame, R. (1995). Shock incarceration and positive adjustment during community supervision. *Journal of Quantitative Criminology, 11,* 111–142.

42. MacKenzie & Souryal (1994).

43. Parent, D. (1989). *Shock incarceration: An overview of existing programs.* NIJ Issues and Practices. Washington, DC: National Institute of Justice.

44. MacKenzie & Souryal (1994).

45. MacKenzie, D., & Donaldson, H. (2004). Boot camp prisons for women offenders. In D. MacKenzie & G. Armstrong (Eds.). *Correctional boot camps: Military basic training or a model for corrections?* (pp. 247–262). Thousand Oaks, CA: Sage.

46. Charges filed in boot camp death. (2006, November 28). Retrieved February 11, 2007 from www.nospank.net/n-q51r.htm.

47. Szalavitz, M. (2006). *Help at any cost.* New York: Riverhead.

48. Williams, S. (2005, April). Zero tolerance (violence in schools). *Child Protection Law Report, 31*(4), p. 36.

49. Ibid.

50. Zero tolerance. (2005, February). *Child Protection Law Report, 31*(2), p. 21.

51. Williams (2005).

52. Ibid.

53. Ibid.

54. Tuzzolo, E., & Hewitt, D. (2006). Rebuilding inequity: The re-emergence of the school-to-prison pipeline in New Orleans. *The High School Journal,* pp. 59–68.

55. Roebuck, K. (2005, May 18). Little trouble-makers land in big trouble. *Pittsburgh Tribune-Review* [Online edition].

56. Bazemore, G. (1997, August). *Balanced and restorative justice for juveniles: A framework for juvenile justice in the 21st century.* Washington, DC: Office of Juvenile Justice and Delinquency Prevention, p. 5.

57. Ibid., p. 5.

58. Ibid., p. 9.

59. Zehr, H. (1990). *Changing lenses.* Scottsdale, PA: Herald Press.

60. Umbreit, M., Greenwood, J., Umbreit, J., & Fercello, C. (2003). *Directory of victim-offender mediation in the U.S.* St. Paul, MN: Center for Restorative Justice and Peacemaking.

61. Bazemore, G., & Day, S. (2002). Restoring the balance: Juvenile and community justice. In W. Palacios, P. Cromwell, & R. Dunham (Eds.). *Crime and justice in America: Present realities and future prospects* (2nd ed., pp. 324–338). Upper Saddle River, NJ: Prentice Hall.

62. Ibid., p. 328.

63. McCold, P. and Wachtel, B. (1998). Restorative Policing Experiment: The Bethlehem Pennsylvania Police Family Group Conferencing Project. Pipersville, PA: Community Service Foundation.

64. McGarrell, W., Olivares, K., Crawford, K., and Kroovand, N. (2000). *Returning justice to the community: the Indianapolis juvenile restorative justice experiment.* Indianapolis: Hudson Institute Crime Control Policy Center.

65. Bright, C. (1997). Net widening. *Restorative Justice Online.* Retrieved 1/15/2007 from www.restorativejustice.org/intro/tutorial/systemic/net.

66. Ibid.

67. Rottman, D., & Casey, P. (2002). Therapeutic jurisprudence and the emergence of problem-solving courts. In W. Palacios, P. Cromwell, & R. Dunham (Eds.). *Crime and justice in America: Present realities and future prospects* (2nd ed., pp. 315–323). Upper Saddle River, NJ: Prentice Hall, p. 317.

68. Ibid.

69. Wexler, D. (n.d.). Therapeutic jurisprudence: An overview. Retrieved January 2, 2007 from www.law.arizona.edu/depts/upr-intj/.

70. Senjo, Scott and Leslie A. Leip. 2001. "Testing Therapeutic Jurisprudence Theory: An Empirical Assessment of the Drug Court Process." *Western Criminology Review* 3(1). [Online]. Available: http://wcr.sonoma.edu/v3n1/senjo.html.

71. Mitchell, D., & Kropf, S. (2002). Youth violence: Response of the judiciary. In G. Katzman (Ed.). *Securing our children's future* (pp. 118–146). Washington, DC: The Brookings Institute.

72. What is a unified family court? (n.d.). *American Bar Association.* Retrieved January 15, 2006 from http://www.abanet.org/unifiedfamcrt/about.html, para. 7.

73. Mitchell & Kropf (2002).

74. Pearson, S. (2004). *Policymakers support youth court growth: Voices and recommendations from the field.* Lexington, KY: National Youth Court Center.

75. Butts, J., Hoffman, D., & Buck, J. (1999, October). *Teen courts in the United States: A profile of current programs.* Office of Juvenile Justice and Delinquency.

76. Benekos, P. & Merlo, A. (2002). Reaffirming juvenile justice. In R. Muraskin & A. Roberts (Eds). *Visions for change* (3rd ed., pp. 265–286). Upper Saddle River, NJ: Prentice Hall.

77. Ibid.

78. Benekos & Merlo (2002).

79. Fishman, S. (2002). *The battle for children: World War II, Youth crime, and juvenile justice in twentieth-century France.* Cambridge, MA: Harvard University Press.

Bibliography

ABA recommends ending "zero tolerance" policies in school. (2001, February 21). *Jefferson City News Tribune* [online edition]. Available at www.newstribune.com/stories/022101/wor_0221010033.asp.

Acoca, L., & Dedel, K. (1998). *No place to hide: Understanding and meeting the needs of girls in the California Juvenile Justice System*. San Francisco, CA: National Council on Crime and Delinquency.

Adler, F. (1975). *Sisters in crime: The rise of the new female criminal*. New York: McGrawHill.

Akom, A. (2001). Racial profiling at school: The politics of race and discipline at Berkeley High. In W. Ayers, B. Dohrn, & R. Ayers (Eds.). *Zero tolerance* (pp. 51–63). New York: The New Press.

Aloisi, M. (2004). Emerging trends and issues in juvenile justice. In B. Hancock & P. Sharp (Eds.). *Public policy, crime, and criminal justice* (3rd ed., pp. 350–364). Upper Saddle River, NJ: Prentice Hall.

Armstrong, G. (2004). Boot camps as a correctional option. In D. MacKenzie, & G. Armstrong (Eds.). *Correctional boot camps: Military basic training or a model for corrections?* (pp. 7–15). Thousand Oaks, CA: Sage.

Austin, J. (1995). The overrepresentation of minority youths in the California Juvenile Justice System: Perceptions and realities. In K. Kempf-Leonard, C. Pope, & W. Feyerherm (Eds.). *Minorities in juvenile justice* (pp. 153–178). Thousand Oaks, CA: Sage.

Ayers, W. (1997). *A kind and just parent: The children of juvenile court*. Boston: Beacon Press.

Bazemore, G., & Day, S. (2002). Restoring the balance: Juvenile and community justice. In W. Palacios, P. Cromwell, & R. Dunham (Eds.). *Crime and justice in*

America: Present realities and future prospects (2nd ed., pp. 324–338). Upper Saddle River, NJ: Prentice Hall.

Bazemore, G., & Schiff, M. (2005). *Juvenile justice reform and restorative justice.* Portland, OR: Willan.

Beales, R. (1985). In search of the historical child: Miniature adulthood and youth in colonial New England. In N. Hiner, & J. Hawes (Eds.). *Growing up in America: Children in historical perspective* (pp. 7–26). Urbana, IL: University of Chicago Press.

Benekos, P., & Merlo, A. (2002). Reaffirming juvenile justice. In Muraskin, R., & Roberts, A. (Eds). *Visions for change* (3rd ed., pp. 265–286). Upper Saddle River, NJ: Prentice Hall.

Bernard, T. (1999). Juvenile crime and the transformation of juvenile justice: Is there a juvenile crime wave? *Justice Quarterly, 16*(2), 337–356.

Billingsley, A., and Giovannoni, J. (1972). *Children of the storm: Black children and American child welfare.* New York: Twyne Publishers.

Bishop, D. (2005). Race and ethnicity in processing. In D. Hawkins, & K. Kempf-Leonard (Eds.). *Our children, their children* (pp. 23–82). Chicago, IL: University of Chicago Press.

Bishop, D. (1996). Race effects in juvenile justice decision-making: Findings of a state- wide analysis. *Journal of Criminal Law and Criminology, 86,* 392–414.

Bishop, D., & Frazier, C. (1988). The influence of race in juvenile justice processing. *Journal of Research in Crime and Delinquency, 25,* 242–263.

Bottcher, J., Isorena, T., & Belnas, M. (1996). LEAD: *A boot camp and intensive parole program: An impact evaluation, second year findings.* Ion, CA: Department of the Youth Authority, Research Division.

Briscoe, J. (2004). Breaking the cycle of violence: A rational approach to at-risk youth. In S. Holmes & R. Holmes (Eds.). *Violence: A contemporary reader* (pp. 259–277). Upper Saddle River, NJ: Prentice Hall.

Brace, C. (1872). *The dangerous classes of New York and twenty years work among them.* New York: Wynkoop and Hallenbeck.

Breckenridge, S., and Abbott, E. (1912). *The delinquent child and the home.* New York: MacMillan.

Bremner, R. (1970–1974). *Children and youth in America* (3 vols.). Cambridge, MA: Harvard University Press.

Bright, C. (1997). Net widening. *Restorative Justice Online.* Retrieved January 15, 2007 from www.restorativejustice.org/intro/tutorial/systemic/net.

Butterfield, F. (2000, September 8). Settling suit, Louisiana abandons private youth prisons. *New York Times,* A14.

Butts, J., Hoffman, D., & Buck, J. (1999, October). *Teen courts in the United States: A profile of current programs.* Office of Juvenile Justice and Delinquency Prevention, Office of Justice Programs. Washington, DC: U.S. Department of Justice.

Caulfield, S. (2000, January). Creating peaceable schools. *Annals, AAPSS, 567,* 170–185.

Charges filed in boot camp death. (2006, November 28). Retrieved February 11, 2007 from www.nospank.net/n-q51r.htm.

Chermak, S. (2003). Marketing fear: Representing terrorism after September 11th. *Journal for Crime, Conflict, and the Media, 1*(1), 5–22.

Chesney-Lind, M. (2001). The juvenile justice system must address the needs of girls. In A. Nakaya (Ed.). (2005). *Juvenile crime: Opposing viewpoints* (pp. 178–186). Farmington Hills, MI: Greenhaven.

Claiborne, W. (1999, December 17). *Study: Racial disparity in school discipline.* Washington, DC: Center on Juvenile and Criminal Justice. Retrieved May 21, 2002, from www.cjcj.org/jpi/washpost121799.

Clapp, E. (1995, March 17). The Chicago Juvenile Court movement in the 1890s. Retrieved October 10, 2006, from www.le.ac.uk/hi/teaching/papers/clapp1. html.

Coontz, S. (2000). The way we never were: American families and the nostalgia trap. New York: Basic.

Crowell, A. (1996, August). Minor restrictions: The challenge of juvenile curfews. *Public Management,* 4–12.

Degler, C. (1980). *At odds: Women and the family in America from the revolution to the present.* New York: Oxford University Press.

DeJong, W., Epstein, J., & Hart, T. (2003). Bad things happen in good communities: The rampage shooting in Edinboro, Pennsylvania, and its aftermath. In M. H. Moore, C. V. Petrie, A. Braga, & B. L. McLaughlin (Eds.). *Deadly lessons: Understanding lethal school violence* (pp. 70–100). Washington, DC: The National Academies Press.

deMause, L. (1988). The evolution of childhood. In L. deMause (Ed.). *The history of childhood: The untold story of child abuse* (pp. 1–73). New York: Peter Bedrick Books.

Deutsch, M. (1993). Educating for a peaceful world. *American Psychologist, 48*(2), 510–517.

Dewey, J. (1899). *The school and society.* Chicago, IL: University of Chicago Press.

Dohrn, B. (2002). The school, the child, and the court. In M. Rosenheim, F. Zimring, D. Tanenhaus, & B. Dohrn (Eds.). *A century of juvenile justice* (pp. 267–309). Chicago, IL: The University of Chicago Press.

Dohrn, B. (2001). "Look out kid, it's something you did": Zero tolerance for children. In W. Ayers, B. Dohrn, & R. Ayers (Eds.). *Zero tolerance* (pp. 89–113). New York: The New Press.

Edelman, P. (2002). American government and the politics of youth. In M. Rosenheim, F. Zimring, D. Tanenhaus, & B. Dohrn, (Eds.). *A century of juvenile justice* (pp. 310–340). Chicago, IL: The University of Chicago Press.

Eisler, R. (2000). *Tomorrow's children.* Boulder, CO: Westview.

Erikson, K. (1966). *Wayward Puritans.* New York: Wiley.

Ezell, M. (1992). Juvenile diversion: The ongoing search for alternatives. In I. Schwartz (Ed.). *Juvenile justice and public policy* (pp. 45–58). New York: Lexington Books.

Federle, K., & Chesney-Lind, M. (1994). Special issues in juvenile justice: Gender, race, and ethnicity. In I. Schwartz (Ed.). *Juvenile justice and public policy: Toward a national agenda* (pp. 165–195). New York: Lexington.

Feld, B. (2005). Race and the jurisprudence of juvenile justice: A tale in two parts, 1950–2000. In D. Hawkins (Ed.). *Our children, their children* (pp. 122–163). Chicago, IL: University of Chicago Press.

Feld, B. (1999). *Bad kids: Race and the transformation of the juvenile court*. New York: Oxford University Press.

Feld, B. (1992). Criminalizing the juvenile court: A research agenda for the 1990s. In I. Schwartz (Ed.). *Juvenile justice and public policy* (pp. 59–88). New York: Lexington Books.

Feld, B. (1988). *In re Gault* revisited: A cross-state comparison of the right to counsel in juvenile court. *Crime and Delinquency, 34,* 393–424.

Feinman, C. (1985). Criminal codes, criminal justice, and female offenders: New Jersey as a case study. In I. Moyer (Ed.). *The changing roles of women in the criminal justice system*. Prospect Heights, IL: Waveland Press.

Ferguson, H. (2004). *Protecting children in our time; Child abuse, child protection and the consequences of modernity*. New York: Palgrave MacMillan.

Finley, L. (2007). Developmental theories. In L. Finley, L. (Ed.). *Encyclopedia of Juvenile Violence*. Westport, CT: Greenwood.

Finley, L., & Finley, P. (2005). *Piss off!* Monroe, ME: Common Courage.

Fishman, L. (2003). "Mule-headed slave woman refusing to take foolishness from anybody": A prelude to future accommodation, resistance, and criminality. In R. Muraskin (Ed.). *It's a crime* (3rd ed., pp. 12–30). Upper Saddle River, NJ: Prentice Hall.

Fishman, S. (2002). *The battle for children: World War II, Youth crime, and juvenile justice in twentieth-century France*. Cambridge, MA: Harvard University Press.

Fox, J., Elliot, D., Kerlikowske, R., Newman, S., & Christenson, W. (2003). *Bullying prevention is crime prevention*. Washington DC: Fight Crime: Invest in Kids. Retrieved November 16, 2006, http://www.fightcrime.org/reports/Bullying Report.pdf 2003.

Frazier, C., & Bishop, D. (1995). Reflections on race effects in juvenile justice. In K. Kempf-Leonard, C. Pope, & W. Feyerherm (Eds.). *Minorities in juvenile justice* (pp. 16–46). Thousand Oaks, CA: Sage.

Gaes, G. (2002). Managing the juvenile offender population through classification and programming. In G. Katzman (Ed.). *Securing our children's future* (pp. 147–174). Washington, DC: The Brookings Institute.

Garland, D. (1990). *Punishment and modern society*. Chicago, IL: University of Chicago Press.

Gauthier, A., & Reichel, P. (1989). *Boot camp corrections: A public reaction*. Paper presented at the annual meeting of the Academy of Criminal Justice Sciences, Washington, DC, March 13–17, 1989.

Getis, V. (2000). *The juvenile court and the progressives*. Urbana, IL: University of Illinois Press.

Gittens, J. (1994). *Poor relations: The children of the state in Illinois, 1818–1990*. Urbana, IL: University of Chicago Press.

Greven, P. (1990). *Spare the child.* New York: Vintage.

Grisso, T. (1981). *Juveniles' waiver of rights: Legal and psychological competence.* New York: Plenum.

Grossberg, M. (2002). Changing conceptions of child welfare in the United States, 1820–1935. In M. Rosenheim, F. Zimring, D. Tanenhaus, & B. Dohrn (Eds.). *A century of juvenile justice* (pp. 3–41). Chicago, IL: The University of Chicago Press.

Guarino-Ghezzi, S., & Loughran, E. (2004). *Balancing juvenile justice.* New Brunswick, NJ: Transaction Publishers.

Hancock, L. (2003, January). Wolfpack: The press and the Central Park jogger. *Columbia Journalism Review, 38,* 38–42.

Hemmens, C., & Barrett, K. (1999). Juvenile curfews and the courts: Judicial response to a not-so-new crime control strategy. In T. Calhoun, & C. Chapple (Eds.). (2003). *Readings in juvenile delinquency and juvenile justice* (pp. 3–20). Upper Saddle River, NJ: Prentice Hall.

Hill, H. (1927). Annual report of the Chief Probation Officer of the Juvenile Court. *Charity Service Reports.* Cook County, Illinois.

Hodgson, L. (1997). *Raised in captivity: Why does America fail its children?* Saint Paul, MN: Graywolf Press.

Holmes, S., & Holmes, R. (2002). *Sex crimes* (2nd ed.). Thousand Oaks, CA: Sage.

Hyman, I., & Snook, P. (1999). *Dangerous schools.* San Francisco, CA: Jossey-Bass.

Inciardi, J. (1996). *Criminal Justice* (5th ed.). New York: Harcourt Brace.

Karlsen, C. (1987). *The devil in the shape of a woman: Witchcraft in colonial New England.* New York: W.W. Norton.

Katz, M. (1968). *The irony of early school reform: Educational innovation in mid-nineteenth century Massachusetts.* Cambridge, MA: Harvard University Press.

Katz, M. (1986). *In the shadow of the poorhouse: A social history of welfare in America.* New York: Basic.

Keeley, J. (2004, December). The metamorphosis of juvenile correctional education: Incidental conception to intentional conclusion. *Journal of Correctional Education, 55*(4), 277–295.

Kempf, K., Decker, S., & Bing, R. (1990). *An analysis of apparent disparities in the handling of Black youth within Missouri's juvenile justice systems.* St. Louis: Department of Administration of Justice, University of Missouri-St. Louis.

Kennedy, D. (1997, March). Juvenile gun violence and gun markets in Boston. *National Institute of Justice.* Retrieved September 30, 2006, from www.ncjrs.gov/pdffiles/fs000160.pdf.

Kennedy, D., Braga, A., & Peihl, A. (2004). *Reducing gun violence: The Boston gun project's Operation Ceasefire.* New York: Diane Publishing Co.

Kobrin, S., & Klein, M. (1982). *National evaluation of the deinstitutionalization of status offender programs: Executive summary.* Washington, DC: U.S. Department of Justice.

Knopfer, A. (2001). *Reform and resistance: Gender, delinquency, and America's first juvenile court.* New York: Routledge.

Krisberg, B. (1998). The evolution of an American institution. *Crime and Delinquency, 44,* 1–5.

Krisberg, B. (1992). Youth crime and its prevention: A research agenda. In I. Schwartz (Ed.). *Juvenile justice and public policy: Toward a national agenda* (pp. 1–19). New York: Lexington.

Krisberg, B., & Austin, J. (1993). *Reinventing juvenile justice.* Newbury Park, CA: Sage.

Lantigua, J. (2003, February 17). Juveniles doin' the time are learning the crime. *Rocky Mountain News* [online edition]. Retrieved February 20, 2003, from www.rockymountainnews.com.

Lathrop, J. (1905). The development of the probation system in a large city. *Charities, 13,* 344.

Lawrence, R. (1998). *School crime and juvenile justice.* New York: Oxford University Press.

Leiber, M. (1994). A comparison of juvenile court outcomes for Native Americans, African Americans, and Whites. *Justice Quarterly, 11,* 257–279.

Leonard, K., & Sontheimer, H. (1995). The role of race in juvenile justice in Pennsylvania. In K. Kempf-Leonard, C. Pope, & W. Feyerherm (Eds.). *Minorities in juvenile justice* (pp. 98–127). Thousand Oaks, CA: Sage.

Lerman, P. (1991). Delinquency and social policy: A historical perspective. In E. Monkkonen (Ed.). *Crime and justice in American history: Delinquency and disorderly behavior* (pp. 23–33). Westport, CT: Meckler Publishing.

Lesko, N. (2002, April 30). Making adolescence at the turn of the century: Discourse and the exclusion of girls. *Current Issues in Comparative Education,* 182–191.

Loeber, R., Farrington, D., Stouthamer-Loeber, M., Moffitt, T., & Caspi, A. (1998). The development of male offending: Key findings from the Pittsburgh Youth Study. *Studies in Crime and Crime Prevention, 3,* 197–247.

Lyons, J. (2001). Mental health service needs of juvenile offenders: A comparison of detention, incarceration, and treatment settings. *Children's Services, 4,* 69–86.

MacKenzie, D. (1990). Boot camp prisons: Components, evaluations, and empirical issues. *Federal Probation, 54*(3), 44–52.

MacKenzie, D. (1997). Criminal justice and crime prevention. In L. Sherman, D. Gottfredson, J. Eck, P. Reuter, & S. Bushway (Eds.). *Preventing crime: What works? What doesn't? What's promising?* Washington, DC: National Institute of Justice.

Mackenzie, D., & Brame, R. (1995). Shock incarceration and positive adjustment during community supervision. *Journal of Quantitative Criminology, 11,* 111–142.

Mackenzie, D., Brame, R., McDowall, D., & Souryal, C. (1995). Boot camp prisons and recidivism in eight states. *Criminology, 33*(3), 401–430.

MacKenzie, D., Gover, A., Styve, G., & Mitchell, O. (2000). *National Institute of Justice research in brief: A national study comparing boot camps with traditional facilities for juvenile offenders.* Washington, DC: National Institute of Justice.

MacKenzie, D., & Parent, D. (2004). Boot camp prisons for young offenders. In D. MacKenzie, & G. Armstrong (Eds.). *Correctional boot camps: Military basic training or a model for corrections?* (pp. 16–25). Thousand Oaks, CA: Sage.

MacKenzie, D., & Rosay, A. (2004). Correctional boot camps for juveniles. In D. MacKenzie, & G. Armstrong (Eds.). *Correctional boot camps: Military basic training or a model for corrections?* (pp. 26–45). Thousand Oaks, CA: Sage.

MacKenzie, D., & Donaldson, H. (2004). Boot camp prisons for women offenders. In D. MacKenzie, & G. Armstrong (Eds.). *Correctional boot camps: Military basic training or a model for corrections?* (pp. 247–262). Thousand Oaks, CA: Sage.

MacKenzie, D., & Souryal, C. (1994). *Multi-site evaluation of shock incarceration: Executive summary.* Report to the National Institute of Justice. Washington, DC: National Institute of Justice.

MacKenzie, D., Styve, G., & Gover, A. (1998). Performance based standards for juvenile corrections. *Corrections Management Quarterly, 2,* 28–35.

Males, M. (1999). *Framing youth.* Monroe, ME: Common Courage.

McCold, P. and B. Wachtel. (1998). *Restorative policing experiment: The Bethlehem Pennsylvania Police Family Group Conferencing Project.* Pipersville, PA: Community Service Foundation.

McCord, J. (1978). A thirty-year follow-up of treatment effects. *American Psychologist, 33,* 284–289.

McGarrell, W., Olivares, K., Crawford, K., and Kroovand, N. (2000). *Returning justice to the community: The Indianapolis juvenile restorative justice experiment.* Indianapolis: Hudson Institute Crime Control Policy Center.

Memmi, A. (1965). *The colonizer and the colonized.* Boston: Beacon.

Mennel, R. (1973). *Thorns and thistles.* Hanover: University of New Hampshire Press.

Miller, A. (1983). *For your own good: Hidden cruelty in childrearing and the roots of Violence* (3rd ed.). New York: Farrar, Straus and Giroux.

Miller, C., & Caputo, M. (2006, October 14). New claims of abuse at boys camp. *The Miami Herald,* pp. 1–2A.

Mintz, S. (2004). *Huck's raft: A history of American childhood.* Cambridge, MA: The Belknap Press of Harvard University Press.

Mitchell, D., & Kropf, S. (2002). Youth violence: Response of the judiciary. In G. Katzman (Ed.). *Securing our children's future* (pp. 118–146). Washington, DC: The Brookings Institute.

Moffat, G. (2003). *Wounded innocents and fallen angels: Child abuse and child aggression.* Westport, CT: Praeger.

Moffitt, T. (1993). "Life-course-persistent" and "adolescent limited" antisocial behavior: A developmental taxonomy. *Psychological Review, 100,* 674–701.

Moore, M. (2006, July 10). Sex crimes break the lock on juvenile records. *USA Today* [online edition]. Retrieved February 7, 2007, from www.usatoday.org.

Morash, M., & Rucker, L. (1990). A critical look at the idea of boot camp as a correctional reform. *Crime and Delinquency, 36,* 204–222.

Morreale, M., & English, A. (2004). Abolishing the death penalty, for juvenile offenders: A background paper. *Journal of Adolescent Health, 35,* 335–339.

Moses, E. (1936). *The Negro development in Chicago.* Washington, DC: Social Science Research Council.

Myers, D. (2005). *Boys among men: Trying and sentencing juveniles as adults.* Westport, CT: Greenwood.

National Center for Juvenile Justice. (2003). *Juvenile arrest rates by offense, sex, and race.* Office of Juvenile Justice and Delinquency Prevention. Retrieved August 8, 2006, fromhttp://ojjdp.ncjrs.org/ojstatbb/excel/JAR_053103.xls.

Newman, K., Fox, C., Harding, D., Mehta, J., & Roth, W. (2004). *Rampage: The social roots of school shootings.* New York: Basic Books.

Operation Ceasefire. (n.d.). Program in Criminal Justice Policy and Management. Retrieved June 12, 2006, from http://www.ksg.harvard.edu/criminaljustice/research/bgp.htm.

Oritz, A. (2004). *Cruel and unusual punishment: The juvenile death penalty, evolving standards of decency.* Washington DC: The Juvenile Justice Center of the American Bar Association.

Orlando, F., & Crippen, G. (1994). The rights of children and the juvenile court. In I. Schwartz (Ed.). *Juvenile justice and public policy: Toward a national agenda* (pp. 89–100). New York: Lexington.

Parent, D. (1989). *Shock incarceration: An overview of existing programs.* National Institute of Justice Issues and Practices. Washington, DC: National Institute of Justice.

Parenti, C. (1999). *Lockdown America.* London: Verso.

Platt, A. (1977). *The Child Savers: The invention of delinquency* (2nd ed.). Chicago, IL: University of Chicago Press.

Platt, A. (1998). The child-saving movement and the origins of the juvenile justice system. In P. Sharp, & B. Hancock (Eds.). *Juvenile delinquency: Historical, theoretical, and societal reactions to youth* (2nd ed., pp. 3–17). Upper Saddle River, NJ: Prentice Hall.

Poe-Hamagata, E., & Jones, M. (2000). *And justice for some.* San Francisco: National Council on Crime and Delinquency.

Polier, J. (1989). *Juvenile justice in double jeopardy: The distanced community and vengeful retribution.* Hillsdale, NJ: Lawrence Erlbaum Associates.

Pollock, L. (1983). *Forgotten children: Parent-child relations from 1500–1900.* Cambridge, MA: Cambridge University Press.

Polsky, A. (1991). *The rise of the therapeutic state.* Princeton, NJ: Princeton University Press.

Popyk, L. (1998, November 9). Luke's tormented world. *Cincinnati Post,* 1.

Press, E., & Washburn, J. (2002). Privatization within the juvenile justice system must be stopped. In A. Nakaya (Ed.). (2005). *Juvenile crime: Opposing viewpoints* (pp. 187–192). Farmington Hills, MI: Greenhaven.

Prothrow-Stith, D. (1991). *Deadly consequences.* New York: HarperPerennial.

Quinn, M., Poirier, J., & Garfinkel, L. (2005). Girls with mental health needs in the juvenile justice system: Challenges and inequities confronting a vulnerable population. *Exceptionality, 13*(2), pp. 125–139.

Reichel, P. (1991). Nineteenth century societal reactions to juvenile delinquents: Preliminary notes for a natural history. In E. Monkkonen (Ed.). *Crime and justice in American history: Delinquency and disorderly behavior* (pp. 103–118). Westport, CT: Meckler Publishing.

Rendleman, D. (1991). Parens patriae: From chancery to the juvenile court. In E. Monkkonen (Ed.). *Crime and justice in American history: Delinquency and disorderly behavior* (pp. 119–173). Westport, CT: Meckler Publishing.

Riok, J. (2006, April). Deadly restraint. Nospank.net. Retrieved February 11, 2007 from www.nospank.net/camps.

Roebuck, K. (2005, May 18). Little trouble-makers land in big trouble. *Pittsburgh Tribune-Review* [Online edition]. Retrieved September 21, 2006, from www.pitts burghlive.com.

Rosenheim, M., Zimring, F., Tanenhaus, D., & Dohrn, B. (Eds.). (2002). *Preface: A century of juvenile justice.* Chicago, IL: The University of Chicago Press.

Rothman, D. (1980). *Conscience and convenience: The asylum and its alternative in Progressive America.* Boston: Little, Brown, and Co.

Rottman, D., & Casey, P. (2002). Therapeutic jurisprudence and the emergence of problem-solving courts. In W. Palacios, P. Cromwell, & R. Dunham (Eds.). *Crime and justice in America: Present realities and future prospects* (2nd ed., pp. 315–323). Upper Saddle River, NJ: Prentice Hall.

Ruddell, R., & Mays, L. (2003). Examining the arsenal of juvenile gunslingers: Trends and policy implications. *Crime and Delinquency, 49,* 231–252.

Salant, J. (2003, March 3). Study finds many teens tried as adults despite inability to understand proceedings. *Rocky Mountain Collegian,* p. 6.

Schlossman, S. (1977). *Love and the American delinquent.* Chicago: University of Chicago Press.

Schlossman, S., & Wallach, S. (1998). The crime of precocious sexuality: Female juvenile delinquency in the progressive era. In P. Sharp & B. Hancock (Eds.). *Juvenile delinquency: Historical, theoretical, and societal reactions to youth* (2nd ed., pp. 41–63). Upper Saddle River, NJ: Prentice Hall.

Schmalleger, F. (2005). *Criminology today* (3rd ed.). Upper Saddle River, NJ: Prentice Hall.

Schneider, E. (1992). *In the web of class: Delinquents and reformers in Boston, 1810s– 1930s.* New York: New York University Press.

Scholle, A. (2000, July). Sex offender registration. *FBI Law Enforcement Bulletin, 69,* p. 17.

Scott, E. (2002). The legal construction of childhood. In M. Rosenheim, F. Zimring, D. Tanenhaus, & B. Dohrn (Eds.). *A century of juvenile justice* (pp. 113–141). Chicago, IL: The University of Chicago Press.

Sealander, J. (2003). *The failed century of the child.* Cambridge: Cambridge University Press.

Secret, P., & Johnson, J. (1997). The effects of race on juvenile justice decision-making in Nebraska: Detention, adjudication, and disposition, 1988–1993. *Justice Quarterly, 14,* 445–578.

Seltzer, T. (2004). Mentally ill youth should not be placed in the juvenile justice system. In A. Nakaya (Ed.). (2005). *Juvenile crime: Opposing viewpoints* (pp. 168– 177). Farmington Hills, MI: Greenhaven.

Senjo, S. & Leip, L. A. (2001). Testing therapeutic jurisprudence theory: An empirical assessment of the drug court process. *Western Criminology Review 3*(1). Retrieved January 9, 2007, from http://wcr.sonoma.edu/v3n1/senjo.html.

Shaw, C. (1966). *The Jackroller.* Chicago: University of Chicago Press.

Sherman, A. (2006, January 17). City seeks to widen sex-offender limits. *The Miami Herald,* pp. 1–2B.

Shoemaker, D. (1996). *Theories of delinquency* (3rd ed.). New York: Oxford University Press.

Simms, S. (1997). Restorative juvenile justice: Maryland's legislature affirms commitment to juvenile justice reform. *Corrections Today, 57,* 94–98.

Slaby, R. (2002). Media violence: Effects and potential remedies. In G. Katzmann (Ed.). *Securing our children's future: New approaches to juvenile justice and youth violence* (pp. 305–337). Washington, DC: Brookings Institute Press.

Slater, P. (1985). "From the *cradle* to the *coffin*": Parental bereavement and the shadow of infant damnation in Puritan society. In N. Hiner, & J. Hawes (Eds.). *Growing up in America: Children in historical perspective* (pp. 27–45). Urbana, IL: University of Chicago Press.

Smith, D. (1985). Autonomy and affection: Parents and children in eighteenth-century Chesapeake families. In N. Hiner & J. Hawes (Eds.). *Growing up in America: Children in historical perspective* (pp. 45–60). Urbana, IL: University of Chicago Press.

Snyder, H., & Sickmund, M. (1999). *Juvenile offenders and victims: 1999 National Report.* Washington, DC: Office of Juvenile Justice and Delinquency Prevention.

Springhall, J. (1998). *Youth, popular culture and moral panics.* New York: St. Martin's Press.

Styve, G., MacKenzie, D., Gover, A., & Mitchell, O. (2000). Perceived conditions of confinement: A national evaluation of juvenile boot camps and traditional facilities. *Law and Human Behavior, 24*(3), 297–308.

Sutton, J. (1988). *Stubborn children.* Berkeley, CA: University of California Press.

Szalavitz, M. (2006). *Help at any cost.* New York: Riverhead.

Tanenhaus, D. (2005). Degrees of discretion: The first juvenile court and the problem of difference in the early twentieth century. In D. Hawkins, & K. Kempf-Leonard (Eds.). *Our children, their children* (pp. 103–121). Chicago, IL: University of Chicago Press.

Tanenhaus, D. (2002). The evolution of juvenile courts in the early twentieth century: Beyond the myth of immaculate construction. In M. Rosenheim, F. Zimring, D. Tanenhaus, & B. Dohrn (Eds.). *A century of juvenile justice* (pp. 42–73). Chicago: The University of Chicago Press.

Teitelbaum, L. (2002). Status offenses and status offenders. In M. Rosenheim, F. Zimring, D. Tanenhaus, & B. Dohrn (Eds.). *A century of juvenile justice* (pp. 158–176). Chicago: The University of Chicago Press.

Teplin, L., Abram, K., McClelland, G., Dulcan, M., & Mericle, A. (2002). Psychiatric disorders in youth in juvenile detention. *Archives of General Psychiatry, 59*(12), 1133–1143.

Testa, F., & Furstenberg, F. (2002). The social ecology of child endangerment. In M. Rosenheim, F. Zimring, D. Tanenhaus, & B. Dohrn (Eds.). *A century of juvenile justice* (pp. 237–265). Chicago: The University of Chicago Press.

The Juvenile Justice and Delinquency Prevention Act of 1974 (n.d.). Retrieved May 21, 2006, from http://www.ncjrs.org/.

Trattner, W. (1970). *Crusade for the children: A history of the National Child Labor Committee and child labor reform in New York state.* Chicago: Quadrangle.

Tuthill, R. (1904). *Children's courts in the United States: Their origin, development, and results.* Washington, DC: Government Printing Office.

Tuzzolo, E., & Hewitt, D. (2006). Rebuilding inequity: The re-emergence of the school-to-prison pipeline in New Orleans. *High School Journal,* pp. 59–68.

Umbreit, M., Greenwood, J., Umbreit, J., & Fercello, C. (2003). *Directory of victim-offender mediation in the U.S.* St. Paul, MN: Center for Restorative Justice and Peacemaking.

Van Waters, M. (1925). The Juvenile court from the child's point of view. In J. Addams (Ed.). *The child, the clinic, and the court* (pp. 217–238). New York: New Republic.

Vito, G., & Simonsen, C. (2004). *Juvenile justice today* (4th ed.). Upper Saddle River, NJ: Prentice Hall.

Walker, S. (2001). *Sense and nonsense about crime and drugs: A policy guide.* Belmont, CA: Wadsworth.

Watkins, J. (1998). *The juvenile justice century.* Durham, NC: Carolina Academic Press.

What is a unified family court? (n.d.). American Bar Association. Retrieved January 15, 2006 from http://www.abanet.org/unifiedfamcrt/about.html.

Wilson, N. (2003). Taming women and nature: The criminal justice system and the creation of crime in Salem Village. In R. Muraskin (Ed.). *It's a crime* (3rd ed., pp. 3–11). Upper Saddle River, NJ: Prentice Hall.

Wolcott, D. (2001, Winter). "The cop will get you": The police and discretionary juvenile justice, 1890–1940. *Journal of Social History.* Retrieved March 19, 2006 from www.looksmarttrends.com/p/articles/mi_m2005/is_2_35/ai?82066734?pi=dyn.

Wood, P., & Grasmick, H. (1999). Toward the development of punishment equivalencies: Male and female inmates rate the severity of alternative sanctions compared to prison. *Justice Quarterly, 16*(1), 19–50.

Wooden, K. (2000). *Weeping in the playtime of others* (2nd ed.). Columbus: Ohio State University Press.

Wordes, M., & Bynum, T. (1995). Policing juveniles: Is there bias against youths of color? In K. Kempf-Leonard, C. Pope, & W. Feyerherm (Eds.). *Minorities in juvenile justice* (pp. 47–65). Thousand Oaks, CA: Sage.

Wu, B. (1997). The effect of race on juvenile justice processing. *Juvenile and Family Court Judges Journal, 48,* 43–51.

Youcha, G. (1995). *Minding the children: Child care in America from colonial times to the present.* New York: Scribner.

Zimring, F. (2002). The common thread: Diversion in the jurisprudence of juvenile courts. In M. Rosenheim, F. Zimring, D. Tanenhaus, & B. Dohrn (Eds.). *A century of juvenile justice* (pp. 142–157). Chicago: The University of Chicago Press.

Index

About the Author

LAURA L. FINLEY is currently Visiting Professor of Sociology at Florida Atlantic University. She is also Manager of the Training Department at Women In Distress, an agency devoted to ending domestic abuse. She is co-author of *Piss Off! How Drug Testing and Other Privacy Violations Are Alienating America's Youth* and *The Sport Industry's War on Athletes*. She is the editor of *Encyclopedia of Juvenile Justice* (Greenwood, 2006).